CATS

Facts, Figures & Fun

"Any book without a mistake in it has had too much money spent on it"

Sir William Collins, publisher

CATS

FACTS, FIGURES & FUN

EVE DEVEREUX

ff&f

This one's just got to be for Danu, Morgan, Muggsy and
Strider, and *in memoriam* Angrboda and Rover.

Cats
Facts, Figures & Fun

Published by
Facts, Figures & Fun, an imprint of
AAPPL Artists' and Photographers' Press Ltd.
Church Farm House, Wisley, Surrey GU23 6QL
info@ffnf.co.uk   www.ffnf.co.uk
info@aappl.com   www.aappl.com

Sales and Distribution
UK and export: Turnaround Publisher Services Ltd.
orders@turnaround-uk.com
USA and Canada: Sterling Publishing Inc. sales@sterlingpub.com
Australia & New Zealand: Peribo Pty. peribomec@bigpond.com
South Africa: Trinity Books. trinity@iafrica.com

A catalogue record for this book is available from the
British Library.

ISBN 13: 9781904332510
ISBN 10: 190433251X

Design (contents and cover): Malcolm Couch
mal.couch@blueyonder.co.uk

Printed in China by Imago Publishing
info@imago.co.uk

CONTENTS

THE MIRACLE FURBALL

It's hard to relate the affectionate little creature rubbing your leg or sprawling on the end of your bed to the notion of a savage predator who's right at the top of Nature's food tree, but cats are among the great miracles of the animal world. Millions of years of evolution have resulted in a creature superbly tailored for its habitat. In the case of the domesticated cat, that habitat has become your home.

The role of a cat within a human family is quite different from that of a dog. The wild ancestors of dogs were pack animals, like modern wolves, and dogs today slot into a human "pack" accordingly, adopting a position in what they perceive as the hierarchy of the human family and developing loyalties to match. (This can lead to problems with some individual dogs, as when they come to believe they're deputy pack leader, in charge when the "pack leader" is away, and thus possibly ready to savage "lesser" pack members who "try to usurp" their perceived role.) Dogs also seem far more demonstrative about their affection, particularly through licking – "kissing". This behaviour arises because newborn puppies lick their mother's mouth to solicit food; this continues into adulthood as a demonstration of allegiance.

By contrast, wild cats are strongly territorial loners, and their domesticated brethren show the same traits. They *adapt* to shar-ing their territory with you and with other cats and to your and the other cats' continued presence – often adapting very thoroughly indeed. Unlike dogs, they do not take readily to training; for a loner, unlike for a pack animal, there is no real comprehension of the notion of obedience to others and no urge to conform or win approval. (Cats are easier to house-train than dogs, however, because their instinct is to excrete well away from the area of their other activities, and to bury the products.)

In effect, domesticated cats regard themselves as belonging to two different species at once: they are humans, in that they're the kittens of human parents who supply food, comfort and affection, while at the same time they are also cats. This dual personality can best be observed in cats who live both indoors and out: the cute, playful, dependent little furball of the indoors can become, as soon as it passes through the cat-flap – or, more particularly, over the garden wall – a completely independent, self-sufficient creature who is, for the size, a pretty fearsome predator. Even more dramatic can be the transformation in a cat who's inside a window should a wild animal or other cat approach from the outside.

The domestic cat can in normal circumstances run as fast as about 40kph (25mph) but when frightened can reach speeds even faster than this: up to about 50kph (30mph). By way of comparison, the fastest human sprinters can reach about 45kph (28mph).

Domestic cats bury their excretions not for reasons of instinctive hygiene but in token of submission to the "bigger cats" of the household – i.e., us. In the wild, the pattern in feline communities is that the local boss tom, far from burying his excrement, piles it up on top of any available prominences. The purpose is that the odours from the excrement will be sensed far and wide, thereby indicating his dominance. Lesser cats in the area will bury their excretions to smother the odours and so indicate their submission. In domestication, all cats have been accustomed since kittenhood to regarding the local humans as surrogate parents and therefore the local bosses.

Cats – like many other mammals, including donkeys and bighorn sheep, as well as some reptiles – possess a sense organ which we do not. Known as Jacobson's organ or the vomeronasal organ, this is essentially an organ of scent, but it would be misleading to think of it as a sort of secondary nose: for one thing, it feeds two different areas of the brain than does the nose – the parts that trigger feeding and certain sexual activities. In the cat this organ is located toward the front of the roof of the mouth.

It's because of this organ that cats display the curious behaviour known as *Flehmen* (the German word has no English equivalent). The cat will touch an object of interest with her/his nose, perhaps also flicking the object a lick, then put the head back and inhale while keeping her/his breath held, usually also wrinkling the nose. The effect is to bring as many scent particles as possible to the vomeronasal organ. The brain then integrates the information from this organ with that received from the nose, and makes its decision accordingly as to how the cat should respond.

There are no heat sensors in a cat's paws, so walking across that hot tin roof would hold no fears for them. They might steer clear of it anyway, though, because otherwise they're far more sensitive to heat than we are.

Cats are far less able to distinguish colours than we are – if they were human, we might describe them as partially colour blind. In general they see colours as much more pastel or washed-out than we do. Consequently, the colour of an object is not an especially important piece of information in the feline world – cat toys are brightly coloured for the sake of the owners, not the cats themselves.

Couple this with the fact that feline vision has a poor ability to distinguish detail (if we could see through a cat's eyes we'd think they were always a bit out of focus) and it might seem that vision is an unimportant sense to cats. Not so: cats' vision is excellent at discerning *movement*, which is why you might see a cat watching with intent interest the flight of an insect that's too small for you yourself to make out except with extreme difficulty.

Cats have an astonishing range of peripheral vision: up to about 285°. Our own peripheral vision covers a range of well below 180°.

Cats are farsighted, and have difficulty seeing things up close. This failing can be to a great extent compensated for by the sensitivity of their whiskers, which convey information to the brain in a way that it's hard for us to imagine. Even a blind cat can sense the position of moving prey via the whiskers detecting the air currents that the prey's motion creates. The information-gathering ability of the whiskers is increased through the upper two rows being able to move independently of the lower two rows.

Cats have difficulty seeing things that are directly under their noses – which is why sometimes they have difficulty finding morsels of food you drop on the floor for them.

Cats quite often act as if they've suddenly heard something, when we think there's nothing to hear at all. This is not because the cat's hearing is especially sharper than ours but because cats can hear a greater range of frequencies than we can – in particular, higher frequencies, in what we would regard as the ultrasonic range. We can hear frequencies as high as only about 20kHz, whereas a cat can hear sounds as high-pitched as 65kHz. Among the ultrasonic sounds of interest to felines are some of the squeaks made by mice behind the walls. It's for the same reason that cats sometimes seem to miaow silently. To the cat it's a perfectly normal miaow; it just happens to be pitched too high for us to hear it.

When cats greet each other, they generally do so by bringing their faces close to each other; if they know each other well, they rub their faces together. In this way they mix the scents produced by the glands at the sides of the mouth and at the temples. It's for very similar reasons that they may sniff each other around the rear end; the scent they're after is not the one you might think but that produced by glands at the base of the tail.

Cats would greet us with a similar face-to-face rub if they could, and often they do when they hop up to join us when we're in bed. When we're standing, though, our faces are far too distant for them to reach with their own. They often attempt to reduce this distance by leaping up onto a piece of furniture or by putting their fore paws against us to stand on their hind legs. Of similar genesis is a behavioural tick you sometimes see: as you enter a room, the cat may greet you with a little half-hop, raising the fore paws as if ready to jump. This could be likened to humans waving in friendly fashion to each other – hand-shaking at a distance, as it were. The cat has no intention of jumping up to rub faces, but is indicating that the emotion's there.

Contrary to popular impression, spaying cats does not stop from them from spraying urine to mark out their territory. It does reduce the frequency of the activity, however; and, more impor-tantly, the odour of the sprayed urine is far less potent, so that we may not notice the smell at all. Other cats, though, recog-nize it all too well.

Another popular misconception is that male cats mark out their territory by spraying in order to warn off other toms. This is not in fact the case: other cats are drawn to the sprayed areas, will sniff it with interest, and will likely add some spray of their own. The odour of the sprayed urine has a considerable information content for a cat: the cat can not only tell which of his old friends have been by recently but also if there are any newcomers in the area – and, for that matter, how long it's been since he himself marked his presence here by a quick spray. Further, sniffing the spray can tell cats a good deal about the physical condition of the sprayer. So really a habitual spraying site for the neighbourhood toms is the feline equivalent of an internet bulletin board: folk drop in every now and then to read the messages of others and to add a message of their own.

The degree of fullness or emptiness of a cat's bladder has no effect on spraying activity: a cat with a full bladder will produce bigger sprays at each site, while a cat with a relatively empty one will deliver smaller packets of urine, or even, if he runs out of available urine altogether, conduct dry sprays – going through all the motions but not in fact spraying anything.

Although domestic cats normally regard us as the parents and themselves as the kittens, in the matter of hunting the roles are, in the cat's mind, reversed. Although somehow, magically, we have access to plenty of food, we're astonishingly dimwitted about hunting: we just can't seem to get the idea.

When a mother cat is rearing kittens she goes through a complicated sequence to educate her brood into the idea of hunting and killing food: first she brings prey to eat in front of them; once she reckons they've got that idea, she'll begin bringing dead prey and demonstrating with it how you deal with live prey; after a couple of weeks repeating that exercise, she will begin leaving the dead prey for the kittens to eat; finally, some while after this, she takes the kittens out for their first hunting expeditions.

Cats obviously reckon we're pretty low on the educated kitten scale. We're still at the stage where they have to bring dead prey to us.

Cats spend only about one-third of their lives awake, in contrast with most other mammals (including us), who spend only about one-third of the time asleep. This curious behaviour of the cat shows how, very early on, the modern cats' ancestors developed as extremely efficient predators: they could catch all the food they needed in a relatively short period of the day, leaving them the rest of their time free for more pleasurable activities – notably, snoozing!

Well fed cats kill just as much prey as hungry ones. The hunting instinct in cats is extremely strong, and there's no need for hunger as a trigger. Among outdoor cats, in fact, well fed individuals are likely to kill *more* prey than hungry ones. This is because the hungry cat will spend much of its time searching far and wide for food, whereas the well fed cat will stick to a single area and happily catch whatever it finds there.

The widely accepted adage that a cat-year is equivalent to seven people-years is a falsehood. The true picture is somewhat more complicated than that.

To calculate the age of your cat in people-years, take as your baseline the fact that a two-year-old cat's age is equivalent to a human age of 24. Thereafter, each cat-year is worth *four* people-years, so a cat who lives to a ripe old age of 21 has achieved the same feat as a human who's made it to the age of 100. (The oldest known cat lived to be 36 years old, which represents about 160 in human terms!)

For cats younger than two years, the arithmetic is obviously rather different – and varies from one cat to the next. Generally speaking, a six-month-old kitten is of equivalent age to a child of 8–10 (although they can be far more sexually precocious than children of this age usually are), and for the succeeding year the cat is going through the equivalent of those tempestuous human years of adolescence – although cat "adolescents" are by and large pleasanter to be around than human ones! Thereafter, things calm down a bit.

Domestic cats (generally) enjoy being stroked because the action mimics the sensation of their being licked by their mother when they were kittens. So far as domestic cats are concerned, humans have taken over the role of the mother – supplying food, warmth, etc. – and the pseudo-lick of a caressing hand is part of this.

Many cats, if stroked or tickled near the base of the spine, respond by sticking their tail straight up in the air. Some people think this is a sexual response, but in fact it reflects the cats' time during kittenhood when their mothers would lick clean their rear ends. Raising the tail out of the way was cooperation, and has become a reflexive action when the base of the tail is touched.

Kittens begin grooming themselves at the age of about three weeks; before then, and perhaps for some considerable while after, the mother grooms her kittens. In adulthood, cats quite often groom each other, primarily as a gesture of friendship but also to some useful purpose – a cat cannot effectively groom the top of her/his own head, for example. Long-haired cats in particular appreciate being groomed by another cat, or perhaps by a human.

Part of the motivation for a cat grooming her/himself is for cleanliness and to rid the fur of tangles, but only part. Grooming serves a number of other functions.

The first of these is tidying the fur so that it all lies in proper order. The fur is a cat's primary temperature regulator – it helps keep the cat warm in cold weather and, less effectively, cool in hot weather. The fur layer is at its most efficient in this when it's well kempt and orderly.

In hot weather, there's an addi-
tional cooling motive for
grooming. Our own bodies
have sweat glands all over the
skin. In hot weather we
perspire, and as the sweat evap-
orates from the surface of the
skin it cools us. (Liquids require
an extra input of energy, called

the latent heat of vaporization, in order to evaporate. The
evaporating sweat draws this heat energy from the body, thus
cooling it.) Cats do not have these sweat glands, but through
grooming they can exploit the same physical process. When
grooming in hot weather they supply a good deal of saliva to
the skin and fur. It's the evaporation of this saliva that cools
the cat.

Cats who've been in the sun have yet another incentive to
groom themselves. The action of sunlight on their fur
produces vitamin D, and thus through licking their fur they
can add extra supplies of this vitamin to their diet.

The tugging at the hairs involved in grooming increases the
secretions of certain glands at the roots of the hairs, and
these secretions have the effect of improving the fur's water-
proofing.

Cats may also groom themselves as a sign of stress — it's something to do to stop themselves from displaying any of the
more orthodox symptoms of anxiety, fear or uncertainty. The
principle's the same as when we make minor adjustments to
our clothing or remove imaginary pieces of lint when we're
put momentarily on the spot, are thinking what we should
say next, and so on.

As noted on page 83, cats also have various reasons for grooming themselves after they've been handled by a human.

It's generally assumed that a cat wags her/his tail when angry,
but this is an oversimplification – cats can often wag their tails
when perfectly happy. What the wagging of the tail indicates is
indecision, which may be a powerful internal conflict –
whether to fight or flee, as in anger – or just the lazy, contented
indecision as to whether to move so a different part can be
petted or just stay still and enjoy the petting that's already in
progress. Tail-wagging is also common in play and games. It
doesn't take much skill for a human to work out which message
is being conveyed.

A more dramatic sign of aggression is the elevation of the hair,
which may not be especially noticeable over the rest of the
body but can turn a sleek, slender tail swiftly into a bristly
brush. If a cat does this while facing up to another cat, you can
be sure that what's about to happen isn't going to be just a play
fight. If the cat does it while facing up to you, there's something
seriously amiss, but now might not be the best time to try to
establish what it is.

Female cats in heat are sexually more insatiable than their male
counterparts, and will eagerly copulate many times in a row. If
their primary partner proves temporarily incapable after the first
few couplings, they may wait until he recovers, but are just as
likely to go after other available males. They may in fact be impreg-
nated by more than one of the males during such a session – the
kittens of a single litter may have several different fathers.

Female cats scream and attack the male as he withdraws after
sex because the cat penis is covered in backward-pointing
spines; the withdrawal thus gives the female a moment of
excruciating pain. This might seem a strange evolutionary adaptation, but in fact the spines have the function of triggering the

female's ovulation, which will start about a day afterwards. Because of this delay, it's the habit of females to copulate as many times as possible – and usually with as many males as possible – during their period of heat: the first day's worth of sexual encounters cannot produce a pregnancy, but thereafter the female will be ovulating and thus ripe for fertilization.

When tom cats grab females by the scruff of the neck during mating they're mimicking the grip mother cats administer on their kittens. They do this because female cats become vicious during sex; however, the females respond to the quasi-bite as they did while kittens, becoming still and cooperative.

The description "sharpening the claws" is misleading when applied to cats' scratching on favoured upright surfaces. What the cat is actually doing is ridding itself of old claw sheaths to make way for new-grown ones that are emerging within the old – rather as a snake sheds its old skin to reveal the new. At the same time, the cat is exercising the muscles associated with the protrusion and retraction of her/his claws. (Both functions, shedding and exercising, are carried out on the hind paws by the cat using the teeth.)

Ideally cats scratch only on the scratching post you've bought at great expense for their use. In practice it can be impossible to persuade individual cats to shift their attentions from a favoured piece of furniture or area of wall. This is because of another, quite unrelated purpose of scratching. Cats have scent glands on the soles of the fore paws, and while scratching they're also scent-marking the place concerned, usually in response to a scent that's already there. In the case of an armchair, this may be *your* scent, with which the cat wishes to mingle her/his own. In the case of a wall, it may be because your wallpaper paste contains animal material. (Cats sometimes become compulsive about licking stamps because of animal matter in the glue.) And so on. You can try to deter unwanted scratching by applying, to relevant areas, smells that the cat doesn't like, or you can try to make the scratching post more appealing by rubbing it with your used underwear. But this may not work: cats may be clawing at their favoured spot because attracted by the scent they themselves have left there earlier.

The cruellest way to stop a cat's unwelcome scratching is declawing front paws. Many vets refuse point-blank to perform this operation, which inflicts considerable pain on the cat. Supposedly kinder declawing techniques have been introduced, but they're "kinder" in the sense that some forms of torture hurt less than others. Even if declawing were painless, it would *still* be unacceptably cruel: a declawed cat is a significantly crippled cat. Imagine if someone proposed to you an operation to amputate all your fingers.

A cat's brain typically weighs 1% of its body weight.

Various researches have shown that the domestic cat has about sixty different vocalizations – with some putting the number as high as a hundred – ranging in volume from a soft purr through miaows and growls up to the full-scale howl. Roaring, however, is confined to just four cat lines, all of them among the big cats: jaguars, leopards, lions and tigers.

Kittens start purring when they are about a week old, and they use purring as a means of communicating to their mother during suckling: a purring kitten is receiving a satisfactory supply of milk, and all is well with the world. At the same time, the mother purrs to reassure the kittens that she's there and has no plans to discontinue the suckling. After weaning, cats purr in what appears to be a bewildering variety of situations, such that the purr can seem to have wildly contradictory meanings: when in pain, when in labour, when perfectly contented, etc. In fact, the meaning is very much the same in all instances: the cat is open to interaction with others – open to being stroked, open to receiving attention to relieve the pain, etc.

Cats and Kittens

Female domestic cats in the Northern Hemisphere usually come into heat in January and June. Pregnancy lasts 64–69 days, with rare pregnancies lasting less or more than this. Females can have kittens as young as about six months; their male counterparts reach breeding age a little later. The number of kittens in the litter can vary very widely, sometimes being just a single infant but more usually in the range three to ten; larger litters are not especially uncommon, with the largest on record being nineteen.

Mother cats usually find somewhere secluded, warm, comfortable and secure in which to give birth. It is wise to try to control where this might be, as otherwise you may find she's made her "nest" in the most improbable place. Putting a blanket-lined cardboard box in a warm, dark, little-used cupboard a couple of weeks beforehand is a good idea; of course, you should make sure the expectant mother knows it's there, and has the chance to familiarize herself with it. Following the birth, the mother may, after the first few weeks, move her brood periodically (every couple of weeks or so, plus or minus) to find a new cozy nook; she does this because, in the wild, the first nest is chosen for security, the second and subsequent ones for the convenience with which prey can be brought to the kittens (see page 12).

You can try to move your cat's brood from any especially unsuitable place she's chosen (in your bed, for example), but don't count on success in this.

The kittens are weaned when they're about two months old, and within about a month of that time the mother may come into heat again. Not for nothing is it a good idea to have cats spayed: friends who might take a kitten from your first litter are unlikely to be quite so cheerful about doing so again a mere five and a half months later.

Kittens are born blind, the eyes beginning to open when the kittens are about ten days old. All kittens initially have blue eyes, whatever colour their eyes will ultimately become.

Very soon after birth, the kittens will start suckling. Interestingly, each kitten will suckle from only one of its mother's teats, and cannot be induced to change to a different one; in those sad instances where a kitten dies, the mother can be left with a full teat because none of the other kittens will suckle from any except the one they've reserved for themselves.

Ideally, kittens should start their interactions with humans as soon as their eyes are open – although of course their mother may not be too keen on you handling her brood. Talking to the kittens and gently stroking them is usually possible, though, and such manoeuvres will serve you well in the cats' adult life; cats raised in catteries, where human contact is minimal, often have great difficulty relating to humans and indeed other cats later. The mother may even allow you to pick the kittens up, although she's unlikely to let them out of her sight.

After weaning, the mother may or may not lose all interest in her kittens, treating them just as she would any other cats in the house. By that time, anyway, the humans of the family should likewise be treating them as independent entities; the earlier they attain their place in the family as a whole, the better for their future happiness.

Thousands of years ago, cats were worshipped as gods.
Cats have never forgotten this.
Anonymous

There are two means of refuge from the
miseries of life: music and cats.
Albert Schweitzer

THE PROVERBIAL CAT

In a cat's eye, all things belong to cats.
England

Those who dislike cats will be carried to the
cemetery in the rain.
Netherlands

If stretching were wealth, the cat
would be rich.
Africa

If you want to know the character of a man,
find out what his cat thinks of him.
England

You will always be lucky if you know how
to make friends with strange cats.
Colonial America

God gave man the cat in order that he might
have the pleasure of caressing a tiger.
France

After dark all cats are cougars.
Zuni (Native American)

To please himself only, the cat purrs.
Ireland

THE TALE
OF THE CAT

While we tend to think of dogs and cats as having been domesticated for about the same – very long – period of time, in fact the cat is a relative newcomer to human society. The first dogs were domesticated well over 100,000 years ago, the first cats, so far as we know, only about 7000 years ago.

A plausible view of the first domestication of cats is that it was coincident with the Agricultural Revolution, meaning that the precise date varied from one human culture to another. The reasoning is that, when humans subsisted as hunter–gatherers, there was little point in recruiting cats as companions. (Dogs, by contrast, were useful hunting assistants.) As soon as people began keeping stocks of grains, however, mice and rats became a problem . . . and what better means of pest-control than adopting a few cats?

A difficulty facing those who've deduced the history of the cat family is that cat fossils differ relatively little from one to the next except in size. Although anatomical comparisons up to about the end of the 20th century were able to paint a fairly good picture of cat evolution, it was only in the early 21st century that this could approach accuracy, thanks to DNA studies.

The 37 species of the cat family, Felidae, originated with a common ancestor in Southeast Asia some eleven million years ago, and from there migrated progressively around the world to every continent except Antarctica. However, the pattern of this migration was not the simple spread one might expect.

About nine million years ago, the ancestral cats migrated across the Bering landbridge from Siberia to Alaska to invade North America; here there emerged the Ocelot, Puma and Lynx lineages. A little while later, cats spread from Asia into Africa, where the Caracal lineage arose. Asia was then repopulated by New World cats, who migrated back across the Bering landbridge, while South America was populated from the continent to its north via the Panama landbridge. The youngest of the eight cat lineages, the one that would eventually lead to the domestic cat, emerged about 6.2 million years ago in Asia and Africa, most probably arising from species that had earlier migrated to North America and then returned to the Old World.

These early migrations were possible because sea levels were low in the period from eleven to six million years ago. Then, however, global sea levels rose and the landbridges were submerged, making further intercontinental migrations impossible. About three million years ago, sea levels dropped once more, and this allowed a further pattern of migrations to develop – most notably, the migration of the American-evolved ancestors of the cheetah and Eurasian lynx from the New World into the Old.

The exceptional spread of cats around the globe was possible because cats have been the second most effective predator of their age – the most effective of all having been humans.

All domestic cats belong to the genus *Felis catus*. The genus *Felis* contains also 26 known species of small wild cats, of which one, *Felis silvestris*, is the species from which the domestic cat derived.

Felis silvestris is a very widespread species, and has three significant races that are physically quite distinct yet obviously of the same species because they interbreed readily. The three are:

* *Felis silvestris silvestris*, European wild cat
* *Felis silvestris libyca*, African wild cat
* *Felis silvestris ornata*, Asiatic wild cat

It seems likely from anatomical comparisons that domestic cats are in fact descendants of only the latter two races, but chromosomally all three races are identical and thus there's no proof that this is so.

Other small wild cats that have been considered as possible ancestors of certain domestic cats are, for Persian cats, Pallas's cat (*Felis manul*) and the Sand cat (*Felis Margarita*), and, for Siamese cats, the Asian golden cat (*Felis temminckii*) and the Leopard cat (*Felis bengalensis*). Pallas's cat and the Leopard cat do have the same chromosomal count as the domestic cat, but anatomical comparisons have ruled all four of these species out of consideration as domestic-cat ancestors.

The Egyptians, who were the first to domesticate wild cats, did also for a period tame the species *Felis chaus*, the somewhat larger Jungle cat, but for one reason or another this practice died out.

A putatively complete listing of small wild cats is:

African wild cat	Andean mountain cat
Bay cat	Black-footed cat
Bobcat	Caracal
Chinese desert cat	European wild cat
Fishing cat	Flat-headed cat
Geoffroy's cat	Iriomote cat
Jaguarundi	Jungle cat
Kodkod	Leopard cat
Marbled cat	Margay
Pallas's cat	Pampas cat
Rusty-spotted cat	Sand cat
Temminck's cat	Tiger cat

Most of the 37 cat species are today either threatened or endangered; the only exceptions are a few small wild cat species and, of course, the domestic cat.

So important were cats as pest-controllers in the agrarian civilization of the ancient Egyptians that they gained an astonishingly high status within society. When a cat died, all the human members of its "family" were obliged to enter full mourning, as if for (say) the family patriarch, and the corpse was embalmed before burial in a wooden coffin in a designated feline cemetery. The penalty for killing a cat was death, and there's on record the case of a Roman soldier who was killed by dismemberment for merely hurting one. The penalties were similarly strict for those caught exporting cats from Egypt. Cats were regarded as creatures worthy of veneration, and the cult of the cat-goddess Bastet (a.k.a. Bast, Ubasti, Pasht), daughter of Isis and Osiris, lasted for some 2000 years – about as long as the cult of Christianity has lasted to date. (It has been theorized that our words "puss" and "pussy" come from the Pasht form of the goddess's name.)

When the British came across the vast ancient-Egyptian cat cemeteries during the 19th century they – notoriously – desecrated them. In one especially philistine example, over 300,000 cat mummies excavated at a temple to Bast on the Nile banks, Tel-Basta (once known as Bubastis), were shipped to Liverpool, England, to be pulverized for use as agricultural fertilizer.

Cats were introduced as house-pets for the wealthy around the Mediterranean by Phoenician traders, who, quite literally risking life and limb, illegally smuggled them out of Egypt. Soon the cats' efficacy in keeping down populations of vermin was discovered, and cats were encouraged at all levels of society. The Romans in particular spread cats all through their territory.

The European Middle Ages represented the nadir for cats. For reasons unknown (and probably not accessible to the rational mind), the established Church developed an antipathy to cats. Using as rationale the notion that cats were servants of the Devil – they had indeed been used in earlier, pagan rituals – the Church instructed the faithful not just to kill cats but to inflict upon them the maximum possible physical suffering: cats were boiled or burnt alive, crucified, flayed . . . Eventually the faithful simply refused to obey these sadistic commands, and after a while the Church quietly dropped them, having caused untold animal suffering in the interim. (Of course, for much of this period the Church was doing equally disgusting things to human beings.) The still-extant superstitions surrounding cats, usually concerning good or bad luck, have their origins in this barbaric era (see pages 28-33).

In the Middle Ages and earlier it was the custom to build a live cat into the foundations of a new building so as to give luck to its occupants.

Cats could not only be witches' familiars, they could also be the witches themselves, shapeshifted into feline form. In 1718 one William Montgomery of Caithness, Scotland, claimed that cats crowded around his house at night and that he could hear them talking to each other in human voices. Further, he told how one night he'd killed two of the cats and wounded another, to find in the morning that two local old women had been found dead in their beds and a third grievously injured. Such tales served as good excuses, if any further excuse were needed by the sadistic folk of the time, to torture and/or put to a hideous death cats and dotty old women alike.

During the English Civil War, Charles I believed that his black cat brought him good fortune, and it was specially guarded. Oddly enough, the day after it died was the day he was arrested.

The concept of cat breeding appears to belong to Victorian England. By the 19th century cats from different parts of the world had developed regional variations in appearance, and English travellers brought home with them foreign cats that took their fancy. Soon the cat-fanciers were breeding the animals to enhance what were deemed desirable features.

CAT SUPERSTITIONS

Black cats are supposedly unlucky in the USA and parts of Europe but supposedly lucky in the UK and Australia. In some regions where black cats are considered lucky, it is white cats who're considered unlucky, and vice versa. In parts of the UK tortoiseshell cats are thought to be lucky, whereas in Russia it's the Russian blue who brings good fortune. In short, superstitions about cat colours – as indeed all superstitions about cats – are a complete muddle, with profound contradictions between one sincerely held folk belief and the next.

The biggest single group of cat superstitions concerns that legendary black cat who crosses your path while you're out walking. The classic version is:

✳ It's bad luck if a black cat crosses your path.

There are lots of variations on this theme. For example:

✳ Conversely, it's good luck if a gray cat or a black-and-white cat crosses your path. Unfortunately, others say that a gray cat crossing your path is a sign of sorrow on the way. And there's a sort of Ascetic School of superstition which decrees that a cat of *any* colour crossing your path is bad luck.
✳ It's particularly unfortunate if you meet the black cat while out walking at night.
✳ Either the bad luck caused by the black cat will befall you during your journey – i.e., you have an accident – or you will be disappointed at the journey's end.
✳ On the other hand, the bad luck may last seven years.
✳ However, if, after the black cat's crossed your path, you find some money on the ground before reaching your destination, you'll have good luck instead.
✳ The bad luck will also be lifted if the cat, having crossed your path once, retraces its steps to cross in front of you again.
✳ Also, you won't be unlucky if the cat is within four feet of you when it crosses your path.
✳ According to a different school of thought, a black cat crossing your path is actually *good* luck, except if it changes its mind halfway and turns back again.

✳ And, according to other experts, it's not the black cat crossing your path that you have to beware: it's if a black cat runs
down the road ahead of you and (this is the important part)
turns right.

✳ Others insist, though, that what you've really got to watch
out for is if it turns *left.*

✳ But the hazards of ambulatory black cats extend further. If
the black cat runs under a ladder, the next person to climb the
ladder will have bad luck.

Just when you thought you'd survived your journey unscathed,
with not a single black cat having been encountered, there's this:

✳ It's bad luck, too, if a big yellow cat crosses your path.

✳ And if a white cat crosses your path it's an omen of sickness
in the family.

You need not take this gratuitous bad-luck delivery lying
down, however. There are various remedies prescribed in
folklore:

✳ After the cat has crossed your path, take twelve steps backward to avert the bad luck.

✳ Some authorities recommend nine steps rather than twelve.

✳ Some say ten is better.

✳ However many backward steps you've taken, it's a good
plan then to turn on your heel.

✳ More drastic backwards walking may be required. Some sages
recommend walking backwards until the cat is out of sight.

✳ Others say you should walk backwards all the way to your
destination, and without speaking.

✳ Alternatively, on seeing the cat ahead of you, turn around
and walk backwards until you've crossed the place where the
cat ran.

For greater security, you may wish to combine backwards
walking with other stratagems:

✳ On seeing the cat, spit on the ground, rub your foot in the
spit, and then take five paces backwards.

✳ Alternatively, make a cross on the ground, take three backward paces, spin round once, and carry on to your destination.

✳ Or walk backwards *ten* paces and spin round *three* times.

Curiously, none of the guides in this matter seem to have thought of an important proviso:

✳ When walking backwards away from the black cat, it is bad luck to do so into heavy traffic.

Bearing this in mind, here are some other possible ways of fending off the bad luck:

✳ As soon as you see the cat, turn your back on it. If, when you next look over your shoulder, the cat's no longer in sight – phew!

✳ Or, on seeing the cat, go straight home and sit down for half an hour before attempting your journey again.

✳ You might get away with turning in the opposite direction from the one you were walking in and continuing your journey by another route, or at least taking a detour.

✳ Or catch the cat and throw it over your left shoulder – though it'd seem this method might in itself bring some dire consequences!

✳ Or you could just spit on your shoes.

✳ Better, though, to spin round three times and then spit on the ground, or your shoes, or both.

✳ Spitting on the first two fingers of your right hand is another recommended practice.

✳ Taking off your hat and spitting into it is yet a further recommended option.

✳ Some prescribe that you stroke the cat three times while reciting the rhyme:

> *Black cat, cross my path,*
> *Good fortune bring to home and hearth.*
> *When I am away from home*
> *Bring me luck where'er I roam.*

✳ Easiest of all, just count to nine.

✳ And, finally, some authorities suggest you can do more than just turn aside the ill cess when a black cat crosses your path.

If you at once look up towards the sky, you will probably find some money before you get home.

There is also a clutch of superstitions concerning cats washing their faces as an indication of imminent guests:

* If a cat starts cleaning her/his face by a door, particularly the front door, visitors will soon be calling.
* Once a cat has finished washing her/his face, if s/he looks to the west there will be visitors coming from the west, if s/he looks to the east there will be visitors coming from the east, and so on.
* When a cat washes her/his face, you can expect visitors to arrive from the direction in which her/his tail is pointing.

Then there are those cats who follow you home:

* If a cat follows you home, that's an indicator of good luck.
* If a cat follows you home, that's an indicator of bad luck. *(Wait a minute! Didn't you just say . . .?)*
* If a white cat comes into your home uninvited, you'll soon have unwelcome (human) visitors.
* A white cat coming to your home is an indicator of good luck, provided s/he stays.
* A black cat coming to your home is an indicator of good luck, provided s/he stays.
* A three-coloured cat coming to your home is an indicator of *especially* good luck, provided s/he stays.
* If you steal a cat and bring it home with you, that's good luck too.
* If you meet a cat in the street and s/he follows you, you'll soon come into some money.
* If a cat comes of its own accord to your house, driving it away will bring bad luck.

In the night all cats are gray.
Miguel de Cervantes

❋ When the first cat was born there was lightning in the sky.

❋ A cat draws lightning to it.

❋ The cat is the only animal that will venture outside when there's lightning in the sky.

❋ Dreaming about a white cat signifies imminent good luck.

❋ If you see a cat dreaming, pull out one of its whiskers and place the whisker under your pillow. That night you'll dream whatever it was the cat was dreaming.

❋ For luck, carry a bone from the left side of a black cat.

❋ For a visitor to kiss the household cat brings good luck.

❋ If you acquire a new cat, bring her/him home blindfolded and throw it onto a bed. Then the cat'll never leave.

❋ Don't let your cat look at her/himself in the mirror, or s/he will run away and leave you.

❋ Confusingly, some advise that, if you want a stray cat to live with you, you should let her/him look in the mirror.

❋ If you rub a stray cat's paws with butter, s/he will never leave you.

❋ The same method averts the bad luck that will otherwise follow should you allow a cat's fur to be blown the wrong way.

❋ To stop a cat running away, cut a little hair from the tail and keep this in your shoes.

❋ If a cat refuses to stay, a death in the family is imminent.

❋ Being scratched by a cat brings bad luck.

❋ If a cat sneezes in the house, bad luck will surely follow.

❋ On the other hand, if the cat of a bride's house sneezes on the day of the wedding, the marriage will be a happy one.

❋ And a further tradition says that good luck will come to all who hear a cat sneeze.

❋ If your cat is killed and you acquire a new one, give the new cat the same name. This will bring good luck.

❋ A cat seen on a grave indicates that the deceased's soul is in the clutches of the Devil.

❋ Two cats seen fighting on a recent grave are the Devil fighting with an angel for the soul of the deceased.

❋ Even worse if you were in Transylvania: if a cat jumped over a grave, the corpse would become a vampire.

❋ It is bad luck to see a cat eating grass.

✻ It is bad luck to step on a cat's tail.
✻ It is bad luck to sleep with a cat. *(Huh?)*
✻ Cats suck the breath from sleeping infants, so that the infants die. *(The allied notion, that cats can smother sleeping infants by sleeping on their faces, appears to be an urban myth born from the fact that some cats will "guard" sleeping babies.)*
✻ A young woman finding a strange cat in her bedroom at night will enjoy good luck.
✻ If you drown a cat, her/his ghost will come back to haunt you . . . and quite right too.
✻ When drowning kittens, always throw them into the water with your left hand – otherwise it's bad luck.
✻ If you have to kill a cat, it's bad luck to do so by drowning.
✻ If you have to kill a cat, it's bad luck to do so by shooting.
✻ If you kill a black cat, you will receive a visit from the Devil before you next see a black cat.
✻ If you drown a cat, your own death will be by drowning.
✻ If you're trying to get rid of a cat *without* killing it, never just put the cat in a sack and dump her/him somewhere. The cat will come home on the ninth day.
✻ To make sure an unwanted cat never returns, carry it away from your home along the side of a stream.
✻ Should you come across a one-eyed cat, make a wish, spit on your thumb, and mark the palm of the other hand with the thumb. Your wish will come true.

Every cat should be given two names, one for public use, one secret, as summarized in the old rhyme:

One for a secret,
One for a riddle –
Name puss twice
To befuddle the Devil.

The secret name is the cat's *real* name. The superstition was that knowledge of someone's real name gave you power over them – and who would seek such power more than the Devil and his minions? Giving the cat a secret name, which witches and the like were too stupid to deduce, protected the cat from being claimed by Evil and thus the household from the possibility of having a tool of Evil in its midst.

THE QUOTEWORTHY CAT

Am writing an essay on the life-history of insects
and have abandoned the idea of writing on
'How Cats Spend their Time'.
W.N.P. Barbellion, *Journal of a Disappointed Man*

The sexophones wailed like melodious cats
under the moon.
Aldous Huxley, *Brave New World*

Cats seem to go on the principle that it never does
any harm to ask for what you want.
Joseph Wood Krutch, *The Twelve Seasons*

You are pictures out of doors,
Bells in your parlours, wild cats in your kitchens,
Saints in your injuries, devils being offended,
Players in your housewifery, and housewives in your beds.
William Shakespeare, *Othello*

Cats, no less liquid than their shadows,
Offer no angles to the wind.
They slip, diminished, neat, through loopholes
Less than themselves.
A.S.J. Tessimond, *Cats*

Cruel, but composed and bland,
Dumb, inscrutable and grand,
So Tiberius might have sat,
Had Tiberius been a cat.
Matthew Arnold, *Poor Matthias*

What is the victory of a cat on a hot tin roof? – I wish I
knew . . . Just staying on it, I guess, as long as she can.
Tennessee Williams, *Cat on a Hot Tin Roof*

One of the most striking differences between a cat and
a lie is that a cat has only nine lives.
Mark Twain, *Pudd'nhead Wilson*

Oh I am a cat that likes to
Gallop about doing good.
Stevie Smith, "The Galloping Cat"

What though care killed a cat, thou hast mettle
enough in thee to kill care.
William Shakespeare, *Much Ado About Nothing*

Some men there are love not a gaping pig;
Some, that are mad if they behold a cat;
And others, when the bagpipe sings i' the nose,
Cannot contain their urine.
William Shakespeare, *The Merchant of Venice*

But thousands die, without or this or that,
Die, and endow a college, or a cat.
Alexander Pope, "To Lord Bathurst"

We [the press] tell the public which way the cat is
jumping. The public will take care of the cat.
Arthur Hays Sulzberger, "On Journalism"

Touch not the cat but [with] a glove.
Walter Scott, *The Fair Maid of Perth*

God is really only another artist. He invented the
giraffe, the elephant, and the cat. He has no real style.
He just goes on trying other things.
Pablo Picasso (*attrib.*)

But the wildest of all the wild animals was the Cat.
He walked by himself, and all places were alike to him.
Rudyard Kipling, "The Cat that Walked by Himself"

Studious of elegance and ease,
Myself alone I seek to please.
John Gay, "The Man, the Cat, the Dog, and the Fly"

When the tea is brought at five o'clock,
And all the neat curtains are drawn with care,
The little black cat with bright green eyes
Is suddenly purring there.
Harold Monro, "Milk for the Cat"

Cats and monkeys – monkeys and cats – all
human life is there!
Henry James, *Madonna of the Future*

I dream
Already that I hear my lover's voice;
What music shall I have – what dying wails –
The seldom female in a world of males!
Ruth Pitter, "Kitten's Eclogue"

It is difficult to obtain the friendship of a cat.
It is a philosophic animal, strange, holding to its habits,
friend of order and cleanliness and one that does not
place its affections thoughtlessly. It wishes only to be
your friend (if you are worthy) and not your slave. It
retains its free will and will do nothing for that
it considers unreasonable.
Théophile Gautier, *La Ménagerie Intime*

CURIOUS AND NOT-SO-CURIOUS CATS

The original cats to be domesticated were probably brownish like the modern *Felis silvestris libyca*, with markings not unlike those we call tabby. The word "tabby" itself may come from "Attabiah", which was the name of the Jewish district in Baghdad famed for the production a particular type of patterned black-and-white silk. This silk was imported to England, where it was called "tabbi", after the district's name. It is likely that the silk's name was then transferred to cat markings of similar pattern, even though usually not of the same black-and-white coloration.

Cat-breeding seems to be almost as old as cat-domestication. Pure tabby markings do not exist in the wild and have to be bred for, yet even in early Egyptian murals, mummy-case decorations, etc., some of the cat depictions appear to show the tabby pattern.

If tabby is the basic pattern of domestic cat markings, it is far from the only one. There are spotted cats, tiger-striped cats, cats all of a single colour (called self-coloured cats by breeders), tortoiseshell cats, and so on. These patterns, along with such factors as hair-length and body-shape, are used to determine the breeds that matter so much to cat-fanciers. Over a hundred different breeds are recognized. Details of them can be found in the appropriate books for breeders and fanciers, but matter not at all to the vast majority of cat-owners, whose beloved animals are free-bred mongrels with coats of any pattern or none. Since mongrels have on average a longer lifespan than purebreds, and are usually less prone to allergies or dietary difficulties, it would seem that the best place for animal-lovers – as opposed to those whose interest is primarily visual – to obtain their cats is by adoption or from a cat shelter, rather than from a specialist cattery. Oddly enough, it is not at all uncommon to come across purebred cats in an animal shelter, desperate for adoption and their existence completely unknown to cat-fanciers.

The two basic divisions in the cat world are *long-haired* and *short-haired*.

———— Short-Haired Cats ————

Abyssinian

The first Abyssinian cats reached the West in the late 1860s, thanks to a British expedition to Abyssinia. Abyssinians are long-bodied and long-necked, and have a wedge-shaped head with large ears. The coat has a banded pattern, the hairs being a ruddy brown tipped with black; the tummy and the insides of the legs are lighter in colour and often have an orange tint. Unusually for domesticated cats, Abyssinians love water and swimming.

The long-haired version of the Abyssinian is considered by cat-fanciers to be a separate breed, known as the *Somali*.

American Short-Hair

Also known as the *domestic short-hair*, this is an attempt to breed back to the cats that came across with the original colonists of the New World. Of course, those colonists knew and cared nothing about cat-breeding – they just brought, you know, *cats* – so the idea of defining this breed by particular features seems a contradiction in terms.

Bobtail
Originally from Japan, these cats have short, pompom-like tails, quite unlike the usual long cat tail. They come in all colours and patterns, but the most prized in Japan are patterned in red, white and black.

British Short-Hair
Slightly smaller and more compact than the American short-hair (q.v.), and with a somewhat larger and sturdier head, the British short-hair comes in all varieties of coloration. Especially notable are the tortoiseshell (sometimes called the *calico*), whose coat is coloured in black plus two shades of red, distributed in distinct patches; and the British blue, which is rather like the Chartreux (q.v.).

Burmese
Quite distinct from the Birman (see page 42), which is a long-haired cat breed that actually came from Burma, the Burmese probably originated in France, with the breed being largely developed in the US, the Siamese component of the ancestry being clearly evident in the body-shape, face-shape and ears.

Chartreux
Originally brought to France from Africa by the monks of Chartreux, these are large cats of a gray-blue coloration and with big, copper coloured eyes. They're unique in the cat world in that they lack the ability to vocalize.

Cornish rex
Often called the *rex cat* or the *poodle cat*, this breed originated by spontaneous mutation in Cornwall, the southwestern tip of England, and is primarily distinguished by its coat, which has the texture you'd expect from the "poodle cat" name. Rather similar but in fact unrelated are the *Devon rex* and the *German rex*, while the New World has the *Oregon rex*.

Exotic Short-Hair
This is a relatively recent US breed produced by crossing the Persian cat, which is long-haired, with the Burmese cat or the

American short-hair. The result is a short-haired cat (the gene for short hair is dominant over that for long hair) with Persian markings.

Foreign Lilac
Known also as the *foreign lavender*, this is essentially the same as a Siamese cat but with fur all of one colour, a very pretty pale lavender.

Havana Brown
Known sometimes in Europe as the *Swiss mountain cat*, this is a breed produced by crossing the Russian blue with the seal-point Siamese. The body-shape is similar to that of the Siamese, with the fur being a sort of smoky brown. The eyes are green.

Korat
Also known as *si-sawat*, this breed originated in Thailand. These cats have a tranquil nature but are also, quasi-paradoxically, fierce fighters. They have large green-gold eyes and a heart-shaped head, but the real distinction is the silver tipping of the body hairs (the breed's name is from the Thai word for "silver").

Manx
Originating in the Isle of Man, an offshore island of the UK, the Manx is distinguished primarily by the fact that it has a slight indentation at the base of the spine where almost all other cats would instead have a tail; for the sake of balance, the cat consequently has heavier hindquarters than most cats. Legend has it that all Manx cats are descendants of an original pair that managed to swim ashore when one of the ships of the Spanish Armada was wrecked in 1588.

Mau
Begun from a pair of imported Egyptian cats in the US, where it is often called the *Egyptian mau*, this breed is primarily distin-guished by the scarab-beetle-shaped markings on the forehead. The cats have long muzzles, slanted yellow or green eyes, and tufted ears. A very similar cat with the same name was bred in

the UK with a rather different genetic heritage. The breed is sometimes called the *ocicat*.

Russian Blue

Sometimes called the *Maltese* or the *Archangel*, this breed probably originated from black cats, the colour diluting over generations to a grey-blue that is shared by both fur and skin. The coat is double, the eyes are green, and the cat is one of those that has a habit of throwing up frequently. Russian blues are often lighter than you expect when you pick them up; this is because the coat doesn't lie flat, so the cat is actually smaller than you think s/he is.

Scottish fold

The distinctive feature here is that the ears, instead of sticking up as in the normal cat, flop over to lie against the side of the head.

Siamese

These were bred in Thailand as sacred temple cats, the breed arriving in the West (in the UK) in the 1880s and very rapidly becoming extremely popular. All purebred Siamese cats have bright blue eyes; a squint is not uncommon. Ideally, to the cat-fancier, the darker areas (*points*) should be confined to the legs, feet, ears, face and tail. The colours of the points are used as classification: blue, frost (a paler version of blue), chocolate, tabby, tortoiseshell, lilac, red or seal, the latter being a rich, dark brown. Siamese cats have a long, thin, athletic body, and they can produce a distinctive, loud bawl that's fairly impossible to describe but which once heard can never be forgotten.

Sphinx

Also known as the *Canadian hairless*, this breed was originated as recently as the 1960s, in Canada. The cats aren't in fact completely hairless, having some on the face, ears and genitalia, but this trivial coverage doesn't affect their suitability as pets for those unfortunate cat-lovers (and there are surprisingly many) who're allergic to cat dander. Sadly, cats of this breed lack whiskers, too, which means they're significantly disabled.

LONG-HAIRED CATS

Angora
The first long-haired cats to reach Europe came from Turkey; this breed derived its name from that of the city of Ankara. The true breed has a completely white coat, although occasionally other colours can be found. The body is much more athletic than that of the Persian (*q.v.*) – longer legs, longer body – and the face shows no Persian-style flattening.

Balinese
Nothing to do with Bali at all, this breed originated in the 1950s in California, where a couple of breeders collected longer-haired Siamese cats and bred them for the length of their coats. Essentially, they're just long-haired Siameses.

Birman
Originating in Burma, where they were supposedly sacred temple cats, the first Birmans arrived in France shortly before 1920, but it wasn't until the 1960s that they impacted the UK and the US. The fur is cream with hints of gold; much darker are the markings, which occupy the same positions as those on Siamese cats. The paws are very distinctive: they're pure white. There seems no connection between the Birman and the short-haired breed called Burmese (see page 39).

Chinchilla
These are all-silver cats, with coloration rather like that of the Andean chinchilla rabbit; the kittens can be born with ringed markings on the tails, but those usually disappear quite soon. These quite delicately built cats were first bred in the UK, around the cusp of the 19th and 20th centuries.

Himalayan
Created by cross-breeding in Europe and the US from the 1930s to the late 1950s between Siamese and Persian cats, this breed combines the coloration of the former with the general coat- and body-type of the latter. The eyes have the same blue as those of Siamese cats, but are the shape and size of a Persian's.

Khmer
The originals of this breed came from Indochina, from around Cambodia, approximately the region ruled by the ancient Khmer people – hence the name. The cats are similar to Birmans (q.v.), but without the pure whiteness of the paws.

Maine Coon Cat
These powerful working cats get their name from the myth that they originated as a cross between domestic cats and raccoons. In reality, they owe their origins to opportunistic mating between the indigenous feline population and long-haired cats brought back by maritime voyagers – conscious human-conducted breeding, with the aim of bringing out the mongrels' best points, being a later development. They are excellent ratters, and are surprisingly big for domestic cats, often exceeding 15kg (27 pounds). They are particularly susceptible to polydactylism – the possession of extra claws.

Persian
Among cat-fanciers, the most popular of all the long-haired

breeds. The Persian has a large head and widely spaced eyes in a face that can be as flat as that of a Pekinese dog. These cats are definitely furballs – they're even furry on the inside of the ears – and their coats can be in any of the feline colours. Persian cats were relatively early arrivals into Europe, coming from Persia (now Iran) as the name suggests, and efforts swiftly began to breed them for luxuriance of coat and flatness of face.

Ragdoll
The ragdoll owes its origins to the work in the 1960s of a California breeder, Ann Baker, who used the kittens of a neighbour's cat. The cat, Josephine, initially half-feral, was involved in a car accident, and during recuperation became much tamer; similarly, the kittens she bore after her accident were far more placid than those she'd borne before. Baker had some very fanciful explanations for this change, including that Josephine had been implanted with human and/or raccoon genes while being operated upon after the accident, and that ragdolls were a sort of missing link between humans and extraterrestrials. (Baker also patented the species and demanded royalties from anyone who bred the cats, an act that created considerable friction between her and the rest of the cat-fancying world.)

Whatever the cause of the change, cats of the breed became and still are astonishingly placid, friendly little furballs. They frequently have the curious habit, when picked up, of going completely limp. Ragdolls can be easily trained to perform tricks like fetch-and-carry and to walk on a leash, and are generally happier with human beings than with other, non-ragdoll cats.

Van Cat
Often known simply as the *Turkish cat*, this breed came originally from Turkey's Lake Van region; it is unusual in that it enjoys water and swimming. Their long, silky fur is primarily white, with auburn markings on the face and tail.

> *The clever cat eats cheese and breathes down rat holes with baited breath.*
> W.C.Fields

CAT-FANCYING SOCIETIES

Fédération Internationale Féline (FIFe)
17 Rue du Verger, L-2665
Luxembourg
http://www.fifeweb.org/intro.html

World Cat Federation e.V.
Geisbergstr.2
D-45139 Essen
Germany
http://www.wcf-online.de/

The International Cat
Association (TICA)
The TICA Executive Office
PO Box 2684
Harlingen
TX 78551
USA
http://www.tica.org/html/english/home/index.php

Co-Ordinating Cat Council of
Australia (CCCA)
Chairperson: Ms Anne Eckstein
MP
Shop 40, Mountain Gate
Shopping Centre
Ferntree Gully
VIC 3156
Australia
http://cccofa.asn.au/

Australian Cat Federation
PO Box 331
Port Adelaide BC
SA 5015
Australia
http://www.acf.asn.au/

Canadian Cat Association (CCA)
289 Rutherford Road, S #18
Brampton, ON
L6W 3R9
Canada
http://www.cca-afc.com/

New Zealand Cat Fancy
Private Bag 6103,
Napier
New Zealand
http://www.nzcatfancy.gen.nz/

Southern Africa Cat Council
PO Box 28732
Kensington 2101
South Africa
http://sacc.ad.co.za/

Governing Council of the Cat
Fancy in the UK (GCCF)
4-6 Penel Orlieu
Bridgwater
Somerset
TA6 3PG
UK
http://ourworld.compuserve.com/homepages/GCCF_CATS/

The Cat Fanciers' Association, Inc.,
PO Box 1005
Manasquan
NJ 08736-0805
USA
http://www.cfa.org/

American Cat Fanciers Association
PO Box 1949
Nixa
MO 65714-1949
USA
http://www.acfacats.com/

CATS IN THE LANGUAGE

One way or another, cats seem to play quite a large part in the English language, with cat-related words and phrases being commonplace. Not all of these are in fact concerned with cats – if you call someone a "pussy" you're not necessarily thinking in a feline context. Here's a mini-guide through at least a few parts of the linguistic labyrinth.

Raining Cats and Dogs
This phrase seems to have become popular in the Middle Ages, when a heavy rainstorm could flood a town. Afterwards, the streets would be littered with the corpses of drowned stray animals, notably cats and dogs, giving the impression these had fallen from the sky. It's unlikely anyone believed this had actually happened, but the illusion must have been a powerful one. Quite why the phrase didn't become "raining cats, dogs and rats" is a mystery.

The Cat Got Your Tongue?
Revoltingly, this phrase dates back to the days when supposed criminals had their tongues cut out and fed to the pets of the local king/lord/tyrant. Thereafter, of course, the victims were mute because a cat – or dog, or whatever – had "got" their tongue.

Letting the Cat out of the Bag

In 18th-century markets, piglets were commonly kept in cloth bags to keep them from running away. (These bags were called pokes; hence the admonition never to buy a pig in a poke.) A well known con trick was to put a cat (relatively worthless) in the bag rather than a piglet, and to claim the "piglet" was too frisky to risk opening the bag for inspection in case the animal escaped. Only the most gullible potential purchasers wouldn't insist, whatever the vendor might say, on opening the bag to take a look.

Not Enough Room to Swing a Cat

The cat concerned was not an animal but the cat-o'-nine-tails, the fearsome weapon with which sailors and others were flogged. Floggings had to be inflicted on deck, because nowhere was there room below to swing the cat. The weapon, a sort of whip with nine metal-tipped lashes, was named after the cat because the wounds it left on the unfortunate victim's back were like those inflicted by a wild cat – although substantially more grievous: it was far from unknown for unfortunates to die of a flogging.

Having Not a Cat's Chance in Hell

At a guess, cats would probably have a better survival chance in Hell than, say, human beings. The form of this phrase that we use today is a contraction of the original: "Having not the chance of a cat in Hell without claws." The allusion was to the unwisdom of being insufficiently armed.

Running a Kitty

Calling a pool of money a kitty is to use a term borrowed from the game of poker, where the kitty is a reserve to which all the players contribute and which is used to pay the house expenses. Poker in turn borrowed the term from prison slang, where it has rather a different meaning: "kitty" is another word for prison. The idea is that the poker-players' money is effectively locked up – it's a reserve no one's allowed to draw on.

An alternative explanation is based on the fact that "kit" was an old word for a small wooden tub or container, which might be thought a suitable item in which to put a group of poker-players' reserve money to keep it separate from the rest.

Being a Cat's Paw, or Catspaw

There's an old tale of a clever monkey that, faced with the challenge of pulling chestnuts from a fire, did so using the paw of a dead cat rather than its own. From this tale arose our expression meaning a dupe, collaborator or brown-noser who lets her- or himself be used as a tool by someone else.

Being at Catty Corners, or Kitty Corners

Both expressions are a corruption of "catercornered", meaning to be diagonally or obliquely opposite – as in two houses being at diagonally opposite corners of a town square. The original term comes from "cater", meaning the four-spot on a die; in turn, "cater" was a corruption of the French word "*quatre*", meaning "four".

Having Kittens

Cats were, in more primitive ages, widely regarded as being witches' familiars. When a pregnant woman suffered undue pain or emotional disturbance, the superstition was that a witch had spelled a litter of kittens into her womb in place of the baby. Since telling a woman she was going to bear a litter of kittens was a sure-fire way to make her hysterical, the superstition was gratifyingly self-reinforcing.

Having Nine Lives

The notion of the cat having more than a single life came about through people observing the way cats survived all kinds of hazards that might easily have done for any other animal: they could fall from great heights and land easily on their feet; they could slip through apertures seemingly too small to allow their passage; and so on. Cats were obviously very lucky, and nine was one of *the* numbers associated with good fortune, being lucky three times lucky three.

Seven is likewise one of *the* wondrous numbers, and so according to some traditions it's seven lives cats have, not nine.

Tom Cats

Until the 1760s male cats were usually referred to as rams. In the year 1760 there was published (anonymously) an exceptionally popular book called *The Life and Adventures of a Cat*. The hero of this tale was Tom the Cat, and the name rapidly became applied to all male cats.

Pussy

The word "puss" probably originated in imitation of the hissing sound one uses to gain a cat's attention: *psst*. Variations are found in most of the European languages. (An alternative explanation is that it comes from the name "Pasht" – see page 26.) In its meaning of "face" the derivation is different: it comes from the Irish *pus*, meaning "lips" or "mouth".

The diminutive "pussy" is presumably of similarly ancient origin; its meaning was occasionally broadened to include other warm and furry animals, in particular the rabbit. The word was first used as an affectionate term for a woman, in the sense of "pussy-cat", before the 1580s; it soon came to be used also, more derisively, for weak-spined or effeminate men. Although nowadays calling someone a pussy is generally thought to be a reference to the female pudenda (see below), in fact the expression is perfectly respectable. In this usage, "pussy" is once more short for "pussy-cat", meaning simply "softy" or "wimp".

The origin of the word's use since at least the 1870s in reference to the female pudenda is more problematic. According to one explanation, it arises from the pre-existent "warm and furry" meaning of "pussy" – as in "pussy willow". An alternative is that in the pudendal sense the word has no cat connotations at all, but instead arises from the Old Norse *puss*, meaning "pocket" or "pouch".

Being the Cat's Pyjamas, Cat's Whiskers or Cat's Miaow

The thought of women wearing pyjamas was initially scandalous – surely only women of ill reputation, such as might be found in cathouses, would do something like that! The expression was thus originally used as an insult rather than in admiration. Among the young flappers of the 1920s, however, being outrageous was regarded as worthy of respect, and so the connotation of the term was turned on its head.

To say that someone thinks of themselves as the cat's whiskers seems to be derived simply from the fact that cats, often regarded as smug, give the impression of being proudest of anything of their whiskers. The reason for calling someone the cat's miaow, however, is a bit harder to unravel. One possibility is that it's a reference to an old British slang term, "cheshire", meaning the correct thing or action. That term *may* have come from the name of Cheshire cheese; a cheeser was someone grinning happily. . . like the Cheshire cat, a folkmyth-figure commemorated in Lewis Carroll's *Alice in Wonderland* (1865). The Cheshire cat was renowned for its smile, and presumably the accompanying miaow.

Kittywompus

In disorder, as per "her hair was all kittywompus". The term seems to belong to that class of words that one might call quasi-onomatopoeic: the sound of the word conveys much of the meaning, in this instance that something is as disordered as if a kitty has been playing in it.

Waiting for a Catpause

A catpause (origins of term unknown, but guessable) is defined as the period of time – measured in small fractions of a second – between someone leaving the room and the people left behind starting to slander (be catty about) the departer.

Schrödinger's Cat

In the first part of the 20th century, as the implications of Quantum Theory began to filter through the scientific consciousness, various scientists – Einstein included – intuitively resisted the newfangled notions, which ran strictly counter to common sense. One of the noncommonsensical notions was Heisenberg's Uncertainty Principle, which states that you cannot simultaneously know all the properties of a particle: if you know its mass, there is necessarily uncertainty about its velocity, and so on, because the very act of making the observation of one property affects the other properties.

By way of a thought experiment, the Austrian–Irish physicist Erwin Schrödinger proposed the notion of a cat put in a closed box with a poison capsule that has a 50% chance of opening, and thus killing the cat, within any given period of time. Schrödinger observed that, until you open the box, you have no way of knowing if the cat is alive or dead, and that therefore, until you do, the cat is *neither* – but instead in an intermediate, indeterminate condition. Only once you've looked inside the box will the cat's condition become one or other of the two absolutes; the observer plays a part in defining the reality. Of course, this statement violates common sense and, on the larger scale of cats and experimenters, violates sanity too; at the fundamental level of reality, however, among the subatomic energy-packets of which the universe is composed, analogues of this situation are the actuality.

The phrase "Schrödinger's Cat" has thus come to mean, through simile, anything that's in an indeterminate state.

People that hate cats, will come back as mice in their next life.
Faith Resnick

A cat isn't fussy – just so long as you remember he likes his milk
in the shallow, rose-patterned saucer and his fish on the blue plate.
From which he will take it, and eat it off the floor.
Arthur Bridges

STAR CATS

Although cats are commonly filled with a certain pride – detractors might call it vanity – at the same time they are in essence modest creatures, content to conceal their genius under a guise of domestic anonymity. Well, sort of. But in fiction, written or otherwise, there have been numerous star cats. Here are a few.

——— CATS OF THE SILVER SCREEN———

There must be several thousand feature movies in which cats feature prominently, almost as many as there are featuring dogs. In addition, there are countless animated feline characters who've appeared in either series of short movies – just think for a start of Tom (in Tom & Jerry), Sylvester, Felix – or full-length features. Often in animated movies cats are nemeses rather than heroes – possibly because mice are so frequently the protagonists.

The Disney animated features are crowded with cats, from Lucifer in *Cinderella* (1950) to Si and Am in *Lady and the Tramp* (1955) to Sergeant Tibs in *One Hundred and One Dalmatians* (1961) to Felicia in *The Great Mouse Detective* (1986), but most especially in *The Aristocats* (1970) and *Oliver and Company* (1988) – and not to forget, however easy it may be to do so, *The Tigger Movie* (2000). Don Bluth followed the Disney trend in

An American Tail (1986), where the cats are the dreaded monster-villains except for the placid, amiable numbskull cat Tiger. Bluth had of course started his post-Disney career as an animator with the short feature *Banjo the Woodpile Cat* (1979).

The animators of Studio Ghibli give cats a more favourable treatment than do, overall, their US counterparts. Cats have incidental roles in many of the movies, but come to the fore in *Whisper of the Heart* (1995) and especially in that movie's quasi-sequel *The Cat Returns* (2002). And who could forget the eponymous heroine's catlike companion in *Nausicaä of the Valley of the Wind* (1984) and most of all the marvellous Cat-Bus in *My Neighbor Totoro* (1988)?

Other animated features that star or co-star cats include, in no particular order:

Ralph Bakshi's *Fritz the Cat* (1972), considered scandalous in its day for depicting a cat with an active sex life and more than a passing acquaintanceship with marijuana.

The Cat in the Hat (1971) is strictly speaking not a feature movie but, at 30 minutes, a featurette. Based on the Dr Seuss children's book, it was remade as a live-action feature in 2003, to little delight.

Cats and Dogs (2001) blends live-action and animation/animatronics in telling about a savage hi-tech cold war that, unknown to humans, wages between the two species.

In the Hungarian movie *Cat City* (1987) there's another ceaseless inter-species war, this time between cats and mice.

In *Gay Purr-ee* (1962) a Parisian chanteuse cat must choose between an honest rustic swain and a slyly manipulating city impresario.

Cats Don't Dance (1997) satirizes Hollywood in a tale of anti-cat prejudice in the movie industry.

The great star of the early shorts was given his own feature in *Felix the Cat: The Movie* (1989). Unfortunately, this was used as the opportunity to make a science fantasy of the dreariest kind. Other classic shorts stars have likewise been given their own feature movies, often as direct-to-video ventures.

Probably the best-known live-action cat movie of all is *Cat People* (1942), a Val Lewton production directed by Jacques Tourneur, in which Simone Simon is sexually frigid because of her fear that, when aroused, she may turn into a wild cat – as did her female ancestors, according to legend. People think it's just that she has a psychological hangup. That proves foolish of them.

The movie was remade in 1982, crassly. Lewton's excellent sequel to the original, this time directed by Gunther von Fritsch, was *Curse of the Cat People* (1944), in which a lonely young girl conjures up the spectre of Simone Simon, her father's dead first wife. A moderately engaging quasi-sequel, not involving Lewton, was *Cat Girl* (1957).

In *Rhubarb* (1951) a cat inherits a Brooklyn baseball team and does a better job than most human team-owners.

Male astronauts travel to the Moon where they discover an underground civilization of man-deprived feline women – yes, it's Hollywood once more showing its respect for the literary values of science fiction, this time in *Cat Women of the Moon* (1954). In a dramatic demonstration of the financial power of dumbness, this was remade a mere five years later, in 1959, as *Missile to the Moon*. The 1954 original is the movie that's so accurately parodied as the backbone of 1987's *Amazon Women on the Moon*.

Shadow of the Cat (1961) returns to the same dark territory as *Cat People*, though thematically and otherwise it's unrelated. A woman is murdered, and her cat takes awesome revenge on the perpetrators.

In Disney's *The Incredible Journey* (1963) a cat and two dogs are companions in venturing through the wilderness to find their lost owners. Disney remade this much later, with slicker technology but arguably less charm, as *Homeward Bound: The Incredible Journey* (1993), which they sequelled in *Homeward Bound II: Lost in San Francisco* (1996).

Disney again: *The Three Lives of Thomasina* (1964), based on a Paul Gallico story, is set in Scotland, in the home of a heartless vet whose daughter loves her cat. Thanks to a mysterious friend's "powers", Thomasina has, if not the legendary nine, at least three lives.

That Darn Cat (1965) is yet another Disney movie, this time a comedy thriller starring Hayley Mills, whose cat brings home a wristwatch that's the key to a kidnapping case. Soon FBI agent Dean Jones, though allergic to cats, is being led by the cat to the unmasking of the plot. Based on the novel *Undercover Cat* (1964) by The Gordons (see page 63). Disney remade the movie in 1997 under the same title, with Christina Ricci in the Hayley Mills role.

Le Chat (1970; a.k.a. *The Cat*) is a French movie based on one of Georges Simenon's psychological novels. Jean Gabin is justifiably disenchanted with his drunken, spiteful wife Simone Signoret, and their cat becomes her rival for his affections – with tragic consequences for the cat.

The chiller *The Cat Creature* (1970), in which a ruthless feline goddess possesses human victims, is based on a script by horror maestro Robert Bloch. It has some thematic affiliation with the 1946 movie *The Cat Creeps*, in which a sinister cat possesses the soul of a dead girl.

No cigars for guessing that *The Cat from Outer Space* (1978) is a Disney movie. This "close encounter of the furred kind" sees an alien cat with paranormal powers (don't all cats have those?) crashland on Earth.

Cat's Eye (1985) is a different kitty of fish altogether: three Stephen King cat-referencing horror stories are linked by the image of a prowling cat. Far more memorable are the vengeful cats in the finale of another Stephen King movie, *Sleepwalkers* (1992).

Oh, look, it's Disney again, this time with *The Richest Cat in the World* (1986), about a talking cat who's inherited a fortune – which, naturally, conniving humans want to extract from his innocent little paws.

"The Cat from Hell" is the central section of three in the port-manteau effort *Tales from the Darkside: The Movie* (1990). A millionaire has to hire a hitman to despatch his supposedly murderous cat. Much of the tale is shown from the cat's view-point.

And Disney's back for more with the TV movie *Murder, She Purred* (1998), based on the Rita Mae Brown and Sneaky Pie Brown series of Mrs. Murphy feline detective novels (see page 60).

After Jim Davis's comic-strip feline creation had featured in quite a number of TV movies, he was finally brought to the big screen in *Garfield* (2004). Garfield's owner Jon brings another pet into the house, a puppy, and the cat's life of lazy luxury becomes a nightmare. But then the puppy is kidnapped and Garfield feels responsible for getting him back ... Surprisingly less dreadful than one might expect.

Halle Berry's performance in *Catwoman* (2004) was not widely appreciated, although some reviewers liked it better, reading the movie as a subversive satire of the whole comic-book super-hero(ine) ethos. Berry wasn't the first to take on the role of Gotham City's slinky feline shapeshifter: previous screen Catwomen have included Eartha Kitt in the 1966–8 TV series, Lee Meriwether in the associated *Batman – The Movie* (1966) and Michelle Pfeiffer in *Batman Returns* (1992).

And never should we forget that so much of the plot of the science-fiction/horror blockbuster *Alien* (1979) is driven not by the alien, not by Ripley, but by the spaceship's cat Jones. In order to get the feline actor to produce the right responses to the alien, the film crew put him in front of a large Alsatian.

The stage musical *Cats*, based on T.S. Eliot's verse collection *Old Possum's Book of Practical Cats* (1939), with music by Andrew Lloyd Webber, was the longest-running presentation in the history of London theatre: it opened on May 11 1981 and ran for exactly 21 years, closing nearly 9000 performances and about £136 million in ticket sales later on May 11 2002. Worldwide, it had by then appeared in about 300 cities in 26 countries, having been translated into 11 languages, with receipts around the $2 billion mark. In New York, the musical's Broadway run ended in September 2000 after 7485 performances.

CAT SLEUTHS AND SLEUTHS WITH CATS

One of the most prolific subgenres of the mystery novel in recent years has been the one featuring cat detectives, or at least involving cats as central characters alongside human detectives. What follows cannot hope to be a comprehensive listing, but hopefully it touches the main bases.

D.B. Olsen
(real name Dolores Hitchens)
An early exemplar in the subgenre, featuring
a feline investigator called Samantha.

Clue in the Clay (1938)
The Cat Saw Murder (1939)
Alarm of the Black Cat (1942)
The Cat's Claw (1943)
Catspaw for Murder (1943)
Cat Wears a Noose (1944)
Cats Don't Smile (1945)
Cats Don't Need Coffins (1946)

Cats Have Tall Shadows (1948)
Cat Wears a Mask (1949)
Death Wears Cat's Eyes (1950)
Something about Midnight (1950)
Cat and Capricorn (1951)
Cat Walk (1953)
Death Walks on Cat Feet (1956)

Lillian Jackson Braun
In ways that are often inscrutable, the Siamese cat Koko, soon joined by paramour Yum Yum, helps a journalist, Qwilleran, solve various murder mysteries. These are
light-hearted tales, like most other cat mysteries.

The Cat Who Could Read Backwards (1966)
The Cat Who Ate Danish Modern (1967)
The Cat Who Turned On and Off (1968)
The Cat Who Saw Red (1986)
The Cat Who Played Brahms (1987)

The Cat Who Played Post Office (1987)
The Cat Who Knew Shakespeare (1988)
The Cat Who Sniffed Glue (1988)
The Cat Who Had 14 Tales (1988) – short stories
The Cat Who Went Underground (1989)
The Cat Who Talked to Ghosts (1990)

The Cat Who Lived High (1990)
The Cat Who Knew a Cardinal (1991)
The Cat Who Moved a Mountain (1991)
The Cat Who Wasn't There (1992)
The Cat Who Went into the Closet (1993)
The Cat Who Came to Breakfast (1994)
The Cat Who Blew the Whistle (1994)
The Cat Who Said Cheese (1996)
The Cat Who Tailed a Thief (1997)
The Cat Who Sang For the Birds (1998)
The Cat Who Saw Stars (1999)
The Cat Who Robbed a Bank (2000)
The Cat Who Smelled a Rat (2001)
The Cat Who Went Up the Creek (2002)
The Cat Who Brought Down the House (2003)
The Cat Who Talked Turkey (2004)
The Cat Who Went Bananas (2004)

Rita Mae Brown and Sneaky Pie Brown
Feline detective Mrs. Murphy tackles a
variety of cases:

Wish You Were Here (1990)
Rest in Pieces (1992)
Murder at Monticello, or Old Sins (1994)
Pay Dirt, or Adventures at Ash Lawn (1995)
Murder, She Meowed (1996)
Murder on the Prowl (1998)
Cat on the Scent (1999)
Pawing Through the Past (2000)
Claws and Effect (2001)
Catch as Cat Can (2003)
Tail of the Tip-Off (2003)
Whisker of Evil (2004)
Cat's Eyewitness (2005)
Sour Puss (2006)

Carole Nelson Douglas
Midnight Louie is the feline detective in this popular and lon-
grunning series, with his human companion being Temple
Barr, a freelance PR. Those marked ★ feature Midnight Louie
on his own; the first two of those four novels are
revised/restored and expanded from *Crystal Days* (1990), the
second two likewise from *Crystal Nights* (1990).

Catnap (1992)
Pussyfoot (1993)
Cat on a Blue Monday (1994)
Cat in a Crimson Haze (1995)
Cat in a Diamond Dazzle (1996)
Cat With an Emerald Eye (1996)
Cat in a Flamingo Fedora (1997)
Cat in a Golden Garland (1997)

Cat on a Hyacinth Hunt (1998)
Cat in an Indigo Mood (1999)
Cat in a Jeweled Jumpsuit (1999)
The Cat and the King of Clubs
  (1999)★
The Cat and the Queen of Hearts
  (1999)★
The Cat and the Jill of Diamonds
  (2000)★

The Cat and the Jack of Spades
  (2000)★
Cat in a Kiwi Con (2000)
Cat in a Leopard Spot (2001)
Cat in a Midnight Choir (2002)
Cat in a Neon Nightmare (2003)
Cat in an Orange Twist (2004)
Cat in a Hot Pink Pursuit (2005)

Lydia Adamson
(real name Frank King)
In the *Alice Nestleton Mysteries* series the eponymous under-
employed actress has a side-job as a freelance cat-sitter, in course
of which she solves mysteries in the company of various cats.

A Cat in the Manger (1990)
A Cat of a Different Color (1991)
A Cat in Wolf's Clothing (1991)
A Cat in the Wings (1992)
A Cat by Any Other Name (1992)
A Cat with a Fiddle (1993)
A Cat in a Glass House (1993)
A Cat with No Regrets (1994)
A Cat on the Cutting Edge (1994)
A Cat on a Winning Streak (1995)
A Cat in Fine Style (1995)

A Cat in a Chorus Line (1996)
A Cat on a Couch (1996)
A Cat under the Mistletoe (1996)
A Cat on a Beach Blanket (1997)
A Cat on Jingle Bell Rock (1997)
A Cat on Stage Left (1998)
A Cat of One's Own (1999)
A Cat with the Blues (2000)
A Cat with No Clue (2001)
A Cat Named Brat (2002)
A Cat on the Bus (2002)

Shirley Rousseau Murphy
Feline sleuth Joe Grey can understand and communicate
with the humans around him, which is handy when it comes
to solving various murders.

Cat on the Edge (1996)
Cat Under Fire (1997)
Cat Raise the Dead (1997)
Cat in the Dark (1999)
Cat to the Dogs (2000)
Cat Spitting Mad (2001)

Cat Laughing Last (2002)
Cat Seeing Double (2003)
Cat Fear No Evil (2004)
Cat Cross Their Graves (2005)
Cat Breaking Free (2006)

Marian Babson
(real name Ruth Stenstreem)

Cats play a significant role in almost all of Babson's crime and
mystery novels. She began early the *Douglas Perkins/Gloria
Tate/Pandora* series in the UK (Pandora being the cat), which
she revived 17 years later when the books were finally picked
up in the US.

> *Cover-Up Story* (1971)
> *Murder on Show* (1972; vt *Murder at the Cat Show*)
> *Tourists are for Trapping* (1989)
> *In the Teeth of Adversity* (1990)

Rather than stick to a single series cat, Babson's relevant
novels (she has written many others) thereafter depict various
feline characters. In *Nine Lives to Murder* the case is solved
by a composite sleuth when a man and cat swap minds.

> *Death Swap* (1984; vt *Paws for Alarm*)
> *A Trail of Ashes* (1984; vt *Whiskers and Smoke*)
> *Nine Lives to Murder* (1992)
> *The Diamond Cat* (1994)
> *Miss Petunia's Last Case* (1996; vt *Canapes for the Kitties*)
> *The Multiple Cat* (1999; vt *The Company of Cats*)
> *A Tealeaf in the Mouse* (2000; vt *To Catch a Cat*)
> *The Cat Next Door* (2002)

Mary Daheim
The adventures of the cat Sweetums:

Fowl Prey (1991)
Just Desserts (1991)
Bantam of the Opera (1993)
Dune to Death (1993)
A Fit of Tempera (1994)
Major Vices (1995)
Murder, My Suite (1995)

Auntie Mayhem (1996)
Nutty as a Fruitcake (1996)
September Mourn (1997)
Snow Place to Die (1998)
Wed and Buried (1998)
Legs Benedict (1999)
Creeps Suzette (2000)

A Streetcar Named Expire (2001)
Suture Self (2001)
Silver Scream (2002)
Hocus Croakus (2003)

This Old Souse (2004)
Dead Man Docking (2005)
Saks & Violins (2006)

The Gordons

This husband-and-wife team came to prominence when their novel *Undercover Cat* was filmed by Disney as *That Darned Cat* (1965); the movie was remade with the same title in 1997.

Undercover Cat (1964)
Undercover Cat Prowls Again (1968)
Catnapped: The Further Adventures of Undercover Cat (1974)

Richard and Frances Lockridge

Various cats participate in the detections of the humans Pam and Jerry North.

Key to Death (1975)
Long Skeleton (1975)
Dead as a Dinosaur (1976)
Voyage into Violence (1976)
The Dishonest Murderer (1978)

The Judge is Reversed (1978)
Murder Comes First (1978)
Death Has a Small Voice (1982)
Curtain for a Jester (1983)
Death of an Angel (1983)

Jeffrey Miller

The Law Society's resident cat, Amicus Curiae, investigates murder mysteries. The author is a well known legal journalist.

Murder at Osgoode Hall (2004)   *Murder's Out of Tune* (2005)

FAMOUS CATS

Chester Willard
As F.D.C. Willard (*Felis domesticus* Chester Willard), this cat became credited with two research papers in low-temperature physics during the 1970s. J.H. Hetherington of the Michigan State University had completed the papers for publication when he discovered that the house-style of the learned journal concerned forbade the use of the auctorial "we". Much simpler than rewriting the papers was to credit his cat as co-author!

CopyCat
The world's first cloned cat – in an experiment by researchers at Texas A & M University in February 2002.

Faith
A cat who received a PDSA Silver Medal for bravery. The church in which she sheltered, St Faith & St Augustine's in London, was bombed during WWII, and Faith nurtured her kitten throughout.

Humphrey
John Major's cat during his tenure as UK Prime Minister. The cat was named for the toadying yet manipulative civil servant Sir Humphrey in the TV series *Yes, Minister*.

Pangur Ban
The cat belonged to the anonymous 8th- or 9th-century Irish monk who penned a poem concerning the similarities between himself and the cat. In the 1980s Pangur Ban became the hero of a series of children's novels by the UK author Fay Sampson.

Cats are intended to teach us that
not everything in nature has a function.
Garrison Keillor

Cats of the Famous

Like it or not, cats usually become famous because of their owners, not in their own right. Here are a few famous owners and some of their cats.

Matthew Arnold
Atossa
> In Arnold's poem "Matthias", about his canary, this three-legged cat featured.

Blacky

The Brontës
Tiger

Winston Churchill
Blackie
Bob
Jock
> Jock received a mention in Churchill's will.

Margate
Mr. Kat/Mr. Cat
Nelson
Tango

Bill and Hillary Clinton
Socks

Colette
La Chatte
La Chatte Dernière
Franchette
Kiki-la-Doucette
Kro
Mini-Mini
Minionne
Muscat
One and Only
Petiteu
Pinichette
Toune
La Touteu
Zwerg

Calvin Coolidge
Blackie/Blacky
Smokey
Tiger
Timmy

R. Crumb
Fred
> The inspiration for Crumb's Fritz the Cat comic.

Charles de Gaulle
Gris-Gris

Charles Dickens
The Master's Cat
William
> William was renamed Williamina when she had kittens!

Benjamin Disraeli
Florence Nightingale

Alexandre Dumas
Le Docteur
Mysouff 1
Mysouff 2

T.S. Eliot
George Pushdragon
Noilly Prat
Pattipaws
Tantomile
Wiscus

John Kenneth Galbraith
Ahmedabad
> *Nicknamed Ahmed, which caused offence when JKB was Ambassador to India, so the name was changed to Gujarat.*

Paul Gallico
Chilla
Chin

Théophile Gautier
Childebrand
Cléopatre
Don Pierrot de Navarre
Enjoras
Eponine
Gavroche
Madame Théophile
Séraphita
Zizi

Ernest Hemingway
Alley Cat
Boise
Crazy Christian
Dillinger
Ecstasy
Fats
Friendless Brother
Furhouse
Mr. Feather Puss/F. Puss
Pilar
Skunk
Thruster
Whitehead
Willy
> *Polydactylism refers to the possession of extra toes. Hemingway became a great fan of polydactylic cats after having been given a six-toed cat by a seafaring friend, and over the course of time reared over sixty of them at his Key West home.*

Thomas Hood
Scratchaway
Tabitha Longclaws
Tiddleywink

Victor Hugo
Gavroche
> *Gavroche was later renamed Le Chanoine, "the canon", because he was so fat and idle.*

Mouche

Samuel Johnson
Hodge
> *Boswell claimed in the* Life *that study of Hodge told a great deal about the mood and character of the irascible Johnson.*

Lilly

Paul Klee
Bimbo
Fritzi
Mys
Nuggi

Edward Lear
Foss

Supposedly an inspiration for "The Owl and the Pussycat"; however, Lear didn't acquire Foss until 1872 and the poem was published in 1871, so this seems unlikely. Foss was certainly, however, the inspiration for "The Heraldic Blazon of Foss the Cat". Foss died in November 1887 and just a few weeks later, in January 1888, Lear himself died.

John Lennon
Elvis

Mohammed
Muezza

On being called to prayer, the Prophet once cut off the sleeve of his robe so as not to disturb Muezza, asleep thereon.

Florence Nightingale
Bismarck
Gladstone

Edgar Allen Poe
Catarina

The inspiration for the short story The Black Cat (1843), and Poe's constant companion.

Cardinal Richelieu
Félimare
Gazette
Lucifer
Ludovic le Cruel
Mimi-Paillon
Mounard le Fougueux
Perruque
Pyrame
Racan
Rubis sur l'Ongle
Serpolet
Soumise
Thisbe

Theodore Roosevelt
Slippers
Tom Quartz

Domenico Scarlatti
Pulcinella

The inspiration for The Cat's Fugue, Pulcinella enjoyed walking along the composer's keyboard. Chopin had a cat with similar predilection, and claimed the animal partly inspired his Valse Brilliante by jumping up on the keyboard midway through the piece's composition.

Albert Schweitzer
Sizi

Robert Southey
Bianchi
Bona Marietta
Catalina
Hurlyburlybuss
Lord Nelson
McBum

Othello
Ovid
Pulcheria
Rumpel
Rumpelstilzchen
Sir Thomas Dido
Virgil
The Zombi

Harriet Beecher Stowe
Calvin

Calvin had the habit of sitting on Stowe's shoulders while she was writing.

Tom Jr

Mark Twain
Apollinaris
Beelzebub
Blatherskite
Buffalo Bill
Satan
Sin
Sour Mash
Tammany
Zoroaster

Queen Victoria
White Heather

THE NURSERY RHYME CAT

Ding Dong Bell

Ding dong bell,
Pussy's in the well.
Who put her in?
Little Johnny Green.
Who pulled her out?
Little Tommy Stout.
What a naughty boy was that
To try and drown poor pussycat.

Hey Diddle Diddle

Hey diddle diddle,
The cat and the fiddle.
The cow jumped over the Moon.
The little dog laughed to see such fun
And the dish ran away with the spoon.

A Cat Came A-Fiddling

A cat came a-fiddling out of the barn
A pair of bagpipes under her arm.
She could sing nothing but, "Fiddle-dee-dee,
The mouse has married the Bumblebee."
Pipe, cat, dance, mouse,
We'll have a wedding at our good house.

Three Little Kittens

Three little kittens
Lost their mittens
And they began to cry.
"Oh, Mother dear,
We sadly fear
Our mittens we have lost!"
"What? Lost your mittens,
You naughty kittens?
Then you shall have no pie."

Three little kittens
Found their mittens
And they began to cry,
"Oh, Mother dear,
See here, see here,
Our mittens we have found."
"What? Found your mittens?
Then you're good kittens,
And you shall have some pie.
Purr, purr,
Purr, purr,
Then you shall have some pie."

As I Was Going To St Ives

As I was going to St Ives,
I met a man with seven wives.
Each wife had seven sacks.
Each sack had seven cats.
Each cat had seven kits.
Kits, cats, sacks, and wives –
How many were going to St Ives?
(Just one: the narrator.)

Mistress Pussy

Six little mice sat down to spin.
Pussy passed by and she peeped in.
"What are you doing, my little men?"
"Weaving coats for gentlemen."
"Shall I come in and cut off your threads?"
"No, no, Mistress Pussy! You'd bite off our heads."

Pussycat, Pussycat

"Pussycat, pussycat, where have you been?"
"I've been to London to visit the Queen."
"Pussycat, pussycat, what did you do there?"
"I frightened a mouse from under her chair."

Dame Trot and Her Cat

Dame Trot and her cat
Led a peaceful life
When they were not troubled
By other people's strife.

When Dame had her dinner
Pussy would wait,
And was sure to receive
A nice piece from her plate.

THE CURIOUS CAT

It was a sad day when, in July 2002, Motor Cat died at the age of 17. She was a cat whose owner, who liked to be known just as Catman, introduced her to the joys of riding with him on his motorbike, which he'd embellished with pieces of carpeting so she could have a more secure grip. She also had a custom-made safety helmet, decorated with her name. After a gradual introduction to this form of transport, Motor Cat became even more enthusiastic about it than her owner, and would urge him to greater speed. The only trouble she had with other drivers was that several were so astonished at the sight of a biker cat that they drove off the road.

Not all cats are so unusual as Motor Cat, but every feline is unusual in one way or another. Furthermore cats are, taken altogether, wonderfully unusual creatures. Here are some things you probably don't know about cats.

Although domestic (and other small) cats cannot roar, like their larger cousins, the big cats cannot purr. Domestic cats purr in a two-way cycle, producing the sound during both inhalation and exhalation. The best that the big cats can manage is a sort of discontinuous half-purr, produced during the exhalation.

White cats are especially susceptible to congenital deafness. A white cat both of whose eyes are blue has a 65–85% chance of being deaf; if one eye is blue and the other a different colour, the odds of the cat being deaf drop to about 40%; and white cats whose eyes are both non-blue have about a 20% chance of being deaf. However, the condition often goes unnoticed, because the deafness may be in one ear only; in this instance, if the cat has one blue and one non-blue eye, the deafness is always in the ear on the same side as the blue eye.

Cats are renowned for their ability to survive long falls, because they are able to twist their bodies as they fall in order to land with all four paws downward, thus absorbing the shock of impact by bending the legs appropriately. Since the contortion takes time, and because the realization that it's necessary likewise takes time, a cat is (within obvious limits) more likely to survive a fall from a higher place than a lower. One study (hopefully not to be repeated) found that cats falling from a twelfth-storey window were 30% more likely to survive than those falling from a sixth-storey window.

In one instance a cat that fell out of a light aircraft survived a drop of well over 300 metres (1000ft).

There are several reasons for thinking that, unlikely as it might seem, cats may originally have learned a good deal of their now-instinctive protective camouflage (if we can extend this term to behaviour) from snakes.

❈ The wild cats most closely related to domestic cats, and thus presumably most like the domestic cat's ancestors, have tabby-like coloration. Further, when cats sleep, they tend to curl themselves into a ball, with the tail wrapped around the outside. The combination of pose and coloration makes a sleeping tabby look not unlike a coiled snake, at least at a quick glance. A quick glance is likely to be as much as a potential predator takes, because most animals give venomous snakes a wide berth.

❈ Similarly, the hiss a cat gives when s/he thinks s/he's threatened is remarkably similar in sound to a snake's hiss. If the potential foe can't see the cat, it might well assume a nearby snake was preparing to strike.

❈ The aural similarity is increased by the cat spitting, again like an aggrieved snake.

❈ Although this may be stretching things a bit, some have

suggested that the flattening of the cat's ears to the skull increases the resemblance of the hissing, spitting head to that of a snake.

❈ Cats preparing to defend themselves habitually move their tails around, again conveying a signal reminiscent of a snake.

Cats' eyes seem to glow in the "dark" (in fact, in the near-dark) because, as part of their adaptation to seeing in very dim light, they have behind the retina a reflecting layer that our eyes do not have. This has the effect of making the maximum use of any light that enters the eyes.

It's a popular myth that cats can't swim. It's just that, with the exception of a couple of breeds (see pages 38 and 44), they don't like water. In fact, when forced into the water they can swim perfectly well. Similarly, they dislike digging into damp soil; if you have a problem with them digging out your house plants, simply keep the earth in the pots as moist as the plant will tolerate.

One marked difference between domestic cats and wild cats is that the domestic cat can hold its tail vertically while walking. Wild cats, by contrast, keep theirs horizontal or tucked between their legs.

Before an electrical storm, cats often wash themselves industriously. This is because at such times the air is charged with static electricity, which transfers itself to the cat's fur (much as happens when you get an electrical shock as you touch a cat). The charged fur attracts airborne dust particles . . . which the cat is diligently removing.

Time spent with cats is never wasted.
Colette

ONE MAN'S MEAT CAN BE A CAT'S POISON

It's a cliché that cats have iron guts and can eat just about anything . . . but, like so many other clichés, this one is not in fact true. Some foods that are quite innocuous or even extremely good for humans are dangerous, and possibly lethal, for cats. Some examples:

Onion – Contains a chemical that attacks the red blood cells in cats, thereby potentially killing the cat through anaemia.

Milk/Cream – Humans possess an enzyme called lactase that helps them metabolize the lactose in dairy products. Kittens possess some, which enables them to metabolize their mothers' milk, but even so they cannot properly metabolize cows' milk. Adult cats are usually wholly deficient in lactase. Thus even moderate quantities of milk, cream or cheese can make a cat seriously ill, or in some instances kill. Those idyllic cats you see lapping up cream in pictures or movies almost certainly suffer, at the very least, severe diarrhoea. Yogurt, however, is okay for cats to eat, while frozen yogurt is a preferable treat to ice cream.

Raw Fish – There are two dangers to cats from eating raw fish. First is an enzyme, present in some fish more than others, that breaks down thiamin and can thereby cause vitamin deficiency. An occasional piece of raw fish as a treat won't do any harm, but the quantity should be kept very small and the intervals betweentimes long. Second, and this applies to cooked fish as well, fish bones are the most dangerous of all to cats, and can kill.

Raw Liver – This has too high a vitamin content for cats to cope with, leading to a condition called hypervitaminosis. Even cooked liver is hazardous in quantity, and thus should be served sparingly and always well/over-cooked.

Canned Tuna – Tuna meals designed for cats are essentially okay, although the cheaper varieties may contain undesirable levels of fat. Feeding a cat canned tuna intended for people, however, is a bad idea, since the tuna will be smothered in either salt water or oil, both of which are harmful to cats.

Raw Eggs – Cats are susceptible to salmonella at far lower doses than humans are. Further, the raw whites contain enzymes that can attack some of the vitamins and thereby encourage skin disorders.

Chocolate – Although some cats like it, chocolate is extremely bad for them, and in quantity can kill. The darker the chocolate, the more dangerous. Other sweetened foods can be harmful as well, at the very least increasing the risk of tooth decay.

Alcohol – A big no-no for cats – see overleaf.

Cats are carnivores. Their digestive systems and metabolisms are set up for a carnivorous diet – i.e., meat/fish/poultry with an admixture of vegetable matter. Unlike humans, who as omnivores can with care switch to a completely vegetarian diet, cats have no such option. Committed vegetarians who attempt to "convert" their cats to vegetarianism merely condemn the animals to considerable suffering and eventual death.

Cats do require some vegetable matter in the diet, primarily for the fibre. In the wild they get some of this from the stomach contents of their prey; in domestication, there's vegetable matter in prepared cat foods. Some cats actively like vegetables, and may be fed small quantities – larger quantities can cause intestinal bloating.

A "vegetable" popular with many cats is grass, which is in fact good for them (although lawn grass may contain pesticides, and so should be avoided). The most important consideration is that the grass contains folic acid, which plays an essential role in the formation of haemoglobin – the chemical that makes red blood cells red. If the cat has insufficient haemoglobin, s/he is likely to become anemic. Of course, grass also contains digestion-aiding fibre and assists in the clearing of hairballs, but these are secondary benefits.

————— CATS AND ALCOHOL —————

There seems to be an affinity between cats and alcohol, and it can be something of a problem. Most often, cats are drawn to beer, which has led to the suggestion that it's the yeasty taste they like; but this hypothesis is shaken by the fact that many cats like cider, and some are known to go for the harder stuff, like whisky.

The problem should not be ignored, or merely laughed off; if a party guest thinks it would be hilarious to give your cat "just a taste", stop them. Cats have difficulty metabolizing alcohol. Tolerances vary from one individual cat to another; in some, quite small amounts can lead to severe vomiting and even coma or death. If the cats have a higher tolerance and regular access to booze, they may become alcoholics, and require to be dried out – preferably under veterinary supervision – as the condition can become terminal.

In Natchez, Mississippi, there is still a statute on the books forbidding the supply of beer to cats.

————— CATS, CATNIP AND POT —————

The effect of catnip (a.k.a. catmint) on cats has often been compared to that of marijuana on people, and the two plants are distantly related. A closer relative to catnip is valerian (*Valeriana officinalis*), which does indeed have a similar effect to catnip's on cats – valerian is, of course, a traditional relaxant and tranquillizer in human herbal medicine. (Catnip can be used similarly.) However, the smell of valerian, which humans simply tolerate, is too offensive for all but the rarest cat to be willing to go anywhere near it. Other herbs that can substitute for catnip are the Japanese plant matatabi (*Actinidia polygama*, a.k.a. silver vine) and *Leriana officialis*, which is a kind of heliotrope.

The active ingredient in catnip is an oil called hepetalactone, which is chemically similar to LSD. As well as giving your cat good vibes, the oil stimulates the same pleasure centres in the brain as does sex. Thus, although catnip oil cannot induce a physiological dependency, there is a slight danger of psychological addiction – which can in rare instances become severe: cats should not be allowed access to unlimited supplies of the stuff.

Since it is the oil that's effective, catnip should always be supplied as fresh as possible. A cat especially fond of catnip can scent the oil in the air when the concentration is as little as one part per billion.

Not all cats like catnip – only about half do – and no one really knows why. It appears that a liking for or uninterest in catnip is genetic, yet this is not an infallible guide – siblings can have different preferences. Likewise, cats can have an adverse reaction to catnip; even a cat who normally enjoys it can on occasion be unlucky.

Although the catnip plant *Nepeta cataria* is related to marijuana, *Cannabis sativa*, the latter plant can be dangerous to cats, causing hallucinations at best, possibly fatal seizures at worst. If you have pot around the house, make sure it's securely kept away from your cat, and keep your cat (and any other pets!) out of any enclosed space in which you smoke it, as even the fumes can cause harm.

The same may be true of tobacco smoke. Although no studies have been done on cats, studies on dogs show an increased susceptibility to lung cancer. A far greater worry with cats is the possibility of their eating a cigarette; the nicotine is of course a poison, and there may be enough in the cigarette to kill them. Nicotine patches, even used ones, represent an even greater hazard.

THE WONDERS OF TOILET TRAINING

Yes, it can be done. There are devices on sale, and they do work, assuming both you and your cat have patience. One alternative approach is this:

* Put the litter tray on a low table or equivalent close to the toilet seat, so that it is at about the same height.
* Once the cat has become accustomed to this, remove the litter tray and secure a piece of strong plastic sheeting between the toilet seat and the porcelain, with a fair amount of the litter in the middle, directly beneath the hole in the seat. You'll need to leave plenty of extra sheeting on all sides, so that, if the cat steps on the litter (as many initially will), the weight won't plunge the cat into the water below. Obviously you need to leave the toilet lid up at all times.
* Retain this situation over a period of a week or two, each day reducing the amount of litter until the cat is using just the plastic.
* Once the cat's okay with this, cut a hole in the plastic.
* And, once the cat's accepted *this*, remove the plastic altogether. If you're lucky, your cat will thereafter balance with four paws on the seat to use the toilet.

———— A LITTERAL HISTORY ————

Cat litter is, surprisingly, a fairly recent invention. For a long time, cat trays were filled with torn-up newspaper, which served but wasn't ideal. Sometime in the 1930s or early 1940s the American entrepreneur George "Poppy" Plitt had the idea of packaging wood ashes, as KleenKitty, for use in cat trays; this was an improvement, but had the disadvantage that cats left sooty pawprints all over the house.

In 1947, a neighbour complained of this to one Edward Lowe. Lowe's father owned a Michigan industrial-adsorbents company, and Lowe suggested to the neighbour that absorbent clay might be the answer. The neighbour tried the clay and was enthusiastic, so Lowe realized there might be a market. His local pet-store owner was sceptical about being able to sell the very first bags Lowe took him, so Lowe told the man to give them away for free. Immediately it became obvious that people were willing to buy the stuff. In due course Lowe took to the road, selling bags of what he had dubbed Kitty Litter from the back of his car. The business escalated, and by 1990 Edward Lowe Industries, Inc., had an annual turnover of $210 million.

In 1984 a biochemist called Thomas Nelson, who'd been investigating the bonding properties of clay, developed the first clumping litter. His breakthrough was realizing that clays that had been dried rather than baked were more absorbent, and would form a clump when wetted. Further, he found that some clays formed hydrogen bonds with the urea molecule so that it did not break down to produce simpler molecules like ammonia, the prime source of urine's smell.

———— MUSICAL CATS ————

At least some cats seem responsive to music, and certainly they can come to recognize a particular piece of music; for example, if you have a favourite television show, and if you have the common habit of petting the cat beside you while watching television, the cat may come to associate the theme tune with the petting. Some people swear that a steady diet of classical music reduces the aggressive instinct in cats; others have noticed that, while many cats run from loud rock music, others are attracted by it (or possibly just by the strong bass rhythm) and will settle down for a tranquil snooze close to the speakers.

Some cats even seem to share human musical sensibilities, in that they'll show signs of distress when music is played out of tune. Mice "sing", and it seems cats are especially attracted to the ones that "sing" out of tune, so it may be that the cat's distress on hearing out-of-tune music arises from the incongruity of there being no accompanying mouse!

Hm. If cats selectively hunt mice that sing out of tune, perhaps we've been wrong about feline motivations all these centuries. It's not that they enjoy killing mice, just that they're doing a public service by silencing the discord. Remember, you read this theory here first . . .

—————— READING A CAT'S EARS ——————

A cat's ears can pivot through a full 180°. The various positions of your cat's ears give considerable information about her/his mental state.

Forward, slightly outward
Relaxed, but still "keeping her/his ears open" for anything of interest.

Directly forward, erect
Alert, intent, focusing on the object of interest. Should a sound of secondary interest start to one side, the cat may swivel the appropriate ear temporarily in that direction, but otherwise the ears remain in the direction of the stare.

Fully flattened
Frightened or apprehensive. This is the defensive position for

the ears, keeping them out of the way of an opponent's teeth and claws in case of a fight.

Partially flattened
The cat is prepared for a fight but is not frightened of the opponent, or is sufficiently aroused to be beyond fear.

Twitching
A nervous response indicating worry or frustration.

One rare piece of behaviour occurs when a cat sees a suitable piece of prey but can't get at it; a typical example would be seeing a bird or a chipmunk through a window. The cat can start to make a very peculiar chattering noise with its jaw. The sound is so very *odd* – and the accompanying grimace is pretty bizarre as well – that it can be quite alarming.

What the cat is doing is mimicking the action it cannot perform, which is delivering the killing bite. When a cat catches prey for food (as opposed to for play), the luckless animal is first pinioned by the claws of the fore feet. In this position it may still be able to fight back – and at that distance a cat's face is vulnerable to attack by even quite small birds and rodents. The cat thus chomps down firmly on the prey's neck to break the spinal cord, immobilizing the creature instantly and killing it within at most seconds. This bite is delivered several times in rapid succession.

Cats are able to know the direction of home, even when removed far from it and by a circuitous route, for the same reason that birds are able to find their way precisely to their homes after their long migratory journeys: they're sensitive to the earth's magnetic field. Even human beings have this sensitivity; we all know people who have "a good sense of direction". It appears the brain can receive information from naturally occurring "magnets" – i.e., iron particles – in the body, and use this information for directional guidance.

The fact that cats can close their eyes to vertical slits reflects their adaptation to nocturnal hunting; coupled with the ability to close their eyelids horizontally (as we do), they have extremely fine control over the amount of light that enters their eyes during daytime, when otherwise they might be blinded by the brilliance. Those species of cats that hunt in the day rather than the night, like lions, have pupils that function the same way ours do.

The gait of cats is unusual in the mammalian world, being shared only by giraffes and camels: the fore and hind legs on one side go forward, one after the other, with the legs on the other side then following suit.

Cats walk so quietly because they do so almost entirely on their toes – on the cushioned pads of their paws. Except when they're at rest, the soles of their feet rarely touch the ground.

—— FELINE DISPLAYS OF AFFECTION ——

Many cat displays of affection are well known and obvious, but others can go unrecognized – even by experienced cat-owners. It's worth noting that purring is not an infallible guide to a cat's state of mind: while it's usually obvious in context if a cat's purring is indicative of happiness, cats can purr in numerous other situations, including pain or distress.

✱ Rubbing ears, face, head or body against you, or wrapping the tail around a part of you – usually done while purring – is the best-known demonstration of affection. The cat is imparting his or her own scent to you, especially from the glands of the face, to show that you're "territory".

✱ If a cat jumps up to sit on your lap, this is a clear sign of acceptance. Comfort plays a part, of course – the lap of a seated human is a warm and luxurious resting place for a cat – but there's more to it than that, since cats are very selective about whose laps they'll grace with their presence. What's not understood is why cats will sometimes jump into the lap of a particular stranger within moments of introduction, even if wary of strangers in general.

✷ Arching the back while rubbing against you or being petted is a strong sign of trust and affection.

✷ Rolling over onto the side or even the back is another indication that your cat is fond of you and trusts you. The cat is exposing the more vulnerable underside of the body for petting and play – something no cat would do if wary of you.

✷ Chirruping. This is a sign of greeting, or of extreme pleasure in your company and/or attentions.

✷ Licking your flesh or clothing. Cats can often groom each other in this way. When cats lick you or your clothing they're in effect grooming you – you're part of the family, an "honorary cat".

✷ Similarly, cats can give you little love-bites or nips, the intent being very similar. It's easy to confuse these with the mock-bites a cat may give you – grabbing a piece of flesh in the mouth but not tightening the grip – to warn you that you're doing something they don't like. Of course, that behaviour too is a sign of affection: otherwise the cat would just bite or scratch you to indicate displeasure!

✷ Kneading you with the forepaws while sitting on your lap or leaning against your chest. This is a behaviour cats first exhibit as kittens, with their mother, so it's feasible you're being treated as a surrogate mother.

✷ Licking fur that you've stroked or petted. This can be misinterpreted by owners as the cat rather waspishly washing and tidying sullied and disordered fur, but in fact the cat is responding affectionately to the scent you've left there – tasting you, as it were. Secondarily, s/he is indeed ordering the ruffled fur; while a third purpose is to remove some of the scent you've left so that the dominant odour is once more the cat's own.

✷ Resting a paw on your hand or wrist while you're tickling or stroking. In part this is to tell you to keep on doing whatever it is you're doing, but cats often lay a paw on you just to demonstrate closeness.

✷ Half-closing the eyes. If a cat, while gazing into your eyes, lazily half- or even more than half-closes the lids, then opens the eyes fully again, this is an overt display of affection.

✳ Holding the tail vertical while with you is a sign of confidence, which implies trust. In general, cats who hold their tails vertical while walking around the house are happy, confident and contented cats.

✳ Bringing you "little presents" of dead animals they've hunted. Obviously the correct, trust-boosting response is delighted acceptance, however sickening the offering.

✳ Turning away from you, lifting the tail upright, and raising the rear end. This is an invitation to you to sniff the glands beside the cat's anus, and no cat could make a kinder offer to you. The fact that no human is likely to *accept* the offer represents a rude rebuff to the cat, and is a major hindrance to cat/human communications.

✳ Stretching, with the fore paws extended as far in front of the head as they'll go, and (assuming the cat is tummy-down on the floor) the back arching up to a raised rear end. Cats lying on their sides will stretch both fore and hind legs to the front and rear, often with a concave arch of the back. A variant is when the cat stretches by standing on the hind legs and putting the fore paws on your leg.

✳ Drooling. Not all cats drool as a sign of extreme pleasure, and those who do this generally do it rarely. Drooling is, like kneading (with which it is often coupled), a reversion to kittenish behaviour.

Do take note if your cat starts drooling outside affectionate contexts: this can be a sign of illness, and so you should go to the vet to have things checked out.

✳ Sleeping with you. The most affectionate of cats may not necessarily choose to sleep on your bed, but those who do are clearly indicating affection. Obviously your body warmth is a big lure, but the cat may also see herself/himself as your guardian, or simply want to be close to you. Some cats will wrap themselves around your feet or head as you sleep, and this can be alarming if they choose to sleep with a baby or small child. (Sleeping infants being smothered by cats seems to be no more than an urban myth.) Cats may also invent affectionate ways of waking you in the morning, such as inserting an extended claw into your nostril and gently p-p-p-plucking!

Cats also have a tendency to display affection preferentially towards strangers who don't like cats. This is thought to be because such people ignore the cats; without the usual gestures and sounds, the cat feels unthreatened by the person. Indeed, one recommended technique of introducing a new cat successfully to your family is, counterintuitively, to ignore her/him entirely until the cat approaches you.

ALLERGIC REACTIONS

People can be allergic to cat hair, but it's rare. The myth that it's the hair that usually causes the allergy arises because hairless cats rarely give rise to allergies in humans. The real cause of almost all cases of cat allergy is the protein in cat saliva. When cats wash themselves – which for obvious reasons hairless cats do much more infrequently than others – the action disturbs dander, which can be thought of as the feline equivalent of dandruff, but with considerably smaller particle size and weight. Bearing protein molecules from the saliva, the dander can float in the air for, quite literally, years.

People with lesser sensitivities to the protein, while they may be undisturbed by the quantities in airborne dander, can still get into difficulties if they stroke a cat. Counterintuitively, they're better off stroking ill kempt cats rather than ones who fastidiously take good care of themselves, because once more the allergy is to the protein in the cat's saliva.

For reasons that aren't completely understood, people can start suffering allergies to cats even after many allergy-free years of cat companionship. Simple acclimatization is presumably the cause of the converse effect, whereby people who suffer an allergic response to cats may gradually cease doing so.

Cats themselves can suffer allergies, and it's estimated that about 15% of them do. Most of these allergies are, as one might expect, to artificial substances they encounter in the human environment – cosmetics, food additives, carpet shampoos, etc. – but not all; for example, the pollen allergy so frequent among humans is shared by some cats. Skin disorders are a common symptom of allergy, especially to foodstuffs; diarrhea, watery eyes, sneezing/coughing and hair loss are others. Of course, all of these may be symptoms of something else entirely, so it's best to consult a vet.

DISEASES FROM CATS

There are perhaps as many as fifty diseases that humans can catch from cats, but the likelihood of so doing is minimal by comparison with your chances of becoming ill through contact with another human being; further, almost all the transmittable diseases can be easily treated . . . if you even notice you've had them at all.

✱ The most common infection is fleas, but even with the most flea-ridden cat the worst you're likely to suffer is an occasional bite; the simplest precaution is, of course, to keep your cat free of fleas.

✱ Cat bites and scratches *can* convey infections because of the germs present in or on the mouth and claws, and they should never be regarded lightly. Treatment of a scratch is simple enough – just wash with the same disinfectant you'd use for any other cut or graze – but, for reasons explained on page 90, a bite may require a visit to the doctor.

✱ Toxoplasmosis is a condition that humans can acquire at second hand via cats; it's caused by the protozoan *Toxoplasma gondi*, and in many instances the problem is so mild that it goes unnoticed . . . but not in all. The consequences of infection can be serious, especially in pregnant woman, because it can be transmitted to the unborn child and cause serious damage to that child's nervous system. In fact, the cat acts merely as a carrier in such cases; the protozoan is acquired through eating prey like mice and birds. If your cat does this, be especially careful when cleaning the litter box and of course handle the remains of the prey with exceptional caution.

✳ The misleadingly named Ringworm is actually a fungal disease, caused by a variety of organisms (athlete's foot and jockrot are related forms). Even cats suffering no symptoms themselves can transmit it to humans; the spores can be transferred by simple contact. There are treatments you can buy to keep your cat free of ringworm, which is the simplest way of preventing the transmission.

✳ Cat scratch fever is rare, but can occur. It's caused by a bacterium called *Bartonella henselae*, which can infect cats – although only briefly – and be transmitted to humans via a scratch. First a pustule forms by the scratched area, then the local lymph glands become inflamed. Usually the fever dies down of its own accord after a month or so; if it persists, medical attention may be required. The best preventative is as before: always treat cat scratches with antibacterial disinfectant.

✳ Outdoor cats can pick up ticks, and these can transfer themselves to humans, thereby imparting genuinely dangerous infections like typhus and Lyme disease, the latter caused by various *Borrelia* spirochete strains which can, less frequently, be transmitted also by mosquitoes, fleas or blackflies. If you spot   a tick on your cat, call the vet for advice – the vet may not appreciate your taking the cat to the surgery. A tick that has already attached itself to your cat is safe enough so far as onward disease transmission is concerned (a tick can transfer the bacterium only once in each cycle), but where there's one tick there may be others hidden in the fur.

✳ Ear mites. It *is* possible for ear mites to pass from cats to humans, but it's exceptionally rare – the researcher who did the main work on this was able to infect himself only with extreme difficulty!

Feline AIDS: Cats can become infected with Feline Immunodeficiency Virus (FIV), which is a close analogue to Human Immunodeficiency Virus (HIV) and causes similar effect in cats. However, the chances of transmission of either FIV or HIV across the species barrier are statistically zero. (Theoretically it's possible, but the likelihood of it ever having happened, or of it ever happening in the future, is vanishingly small.) Cats can infect other cats, though, in much the same ways as humans can pass HIV on to each other, so once the condition has been diagnosed the infected cat should be isolated immediately; thereafter the kindest thing to do is probably put the cat down. Before adopting stray cats, it is wise to have them tested by your vet for FIV.

Mad Cat Disease: During the BSE outbreaks of the 1990s there were a few cases in Europe of cats catching the feline version of the disease from canned cat food that contained diseased beef. The chances of this occurring there again are zero, now that the drastic culling of British herds has been carried out and the disease (hopefully) eliminated from them. In the USA, where there has been considerable denial about the prevalence of BSE in the herds, there would appear at first glance still to be a chance of a cat being infected by the disease. However, the regulations (currently) governing the processing of pet food seem to obviate that possibility, since they require temperatures high enough to destroy or at least disable the prion responsible.

A Dangerous Bite: Up to 50% of the wounds caused by a cat bite may become infectious, a far higher percentage than for dogs. This is not because cats' mouths are less hygienic than dogs' – they're about the same – but because of the shape of the teeth. Dogs have broader teeth, so the wounds are open, relatively easily cleaned, and anyway more susceptible to being flushed out by the flow of blood. Cats' teeth, however, being near needle-sharp, tend to inject the germs under the skin, creating little of the bleeding that would help cleanse the wound.

It may seem a mystery as to why – classically – the cat who gets *up* a tree can't then get *down* it again. It's not because cats are scared of heights, or any such myth, but because all the claws on a cat's feet, front and back, point backwards. This means that they're ideally disposed for digging into (say) bark on the upward climb, but absolutely useless for downward climbing . . . unless the cat works out that s/he should descend backwards, which very, very few cats do.

———— RESPONDING TO DOGS ————

The cliché from comics and movies is of the dog and cat forming a single blurred streak as the former chases the latter, but in real life this is not especially common. Most often, the cat stands up to the dog, who usually decides to beat a strategic retreat. This is because cats have generally learned early on that running from a dog is a very bad idea: the flight stimulates the dog's hunting instinct, and it may be very difficult indeed for the cat thereafter to shake itself free of the dog's attentions – and, should the dog then actually catch the cat, the consequence may easily be fatal.

In some instances, cats deliberately exploit this instinct of the dog, inducing the dog to chase them until it finds itself in a vulnerable position. In one example known to the author, a cat ran from an extremely aggressive bulldog to a mesh fence, over which the cat leapt, then waited. The dog jammed its nose through one of the apertures in the mesh, whereupon the cat slashed its face to ribbons. One trip to the vet later there was a bulldog that had abandoned for life its habit of terrorizing the neighbourhood . . . and which certainly never chased a cat again.

Most usually, though, as noted, cats face down dogs. They typically do so by arching the back, puffing up the fur and turning sideways, all so as to present the largest possible profile to the dog, while hissing a warning. The posture is interesting. When cats prepare to fight each other, the aggressor walks forward on stiff legs and with a straight back while the defender crouches low to the ground, arching the back. The display towards a dog combines the two elements, showing that, while the cat is frightened, s/he is prepared to be the aggressor.

PLAYING WITH PREY

Cats in the wild do not play with the smaller animals they've caught; the behaviour is specific to the domestic cat. There are two quite distinct forms of play with prey, and they arise for different reasons. In both instances, they have their roots in the fact that domestic cats, especially those living entirely indoors, have very little opportunity for hunting.

✱ In one form of "play" the cat catches the mouse and then releases it, then chases it again – perhaps running around for a while betweentimes with the mouse held gently in her/his mouth. In this type of play the cat, whose hunting instinct has had no outlet for perhaps years, is deliberately prolonging the hunt. Hence the look of profound disappointment cats can adopt when, as often happens, the mouse dies of a heart attack before the cat has "formally" killed it by delivering the killing bite (see page 83). Hence, too, the way the cat may prod and poke the mouse for some while after death: the cat's hoping the victim will revive so the chase can continue.

✱ The second form of "play" involves whopping the still-living prey around with the fore paws, claws extended. In the wild, some of the prey cats catch can be quite capable of dangerous, even lethal, retaliation while the cat's attempting to deliver the killing bite. What the cat does to reduce this risk is, essentially, to beat the prey up so that it's in no condition to retaliate as the cat's vulnerable face approaches for the kill. Domestic cats, unaccustomed to hunting, perform this behaviour on inappropriate occasions – as when the prey is too small to do much damage – and for an inappropriate length of time.

The typical miaow of the cat is in fact reserved almost exclusively for communication with humans. Cats rarely miaow at other cats except, when they're kittens, at their mothers. Once

again this is a sign that domestic cats regard their owners as surrogate mothers.

Cats lap water using the underside of the tongue, rather than using the tongue as a spoon-like scoop. The process is difficult to describe: the best idea is to watch closely the next time your cat approaches the water bowl.

Completely black cats are relatively rare – almost all of them feature some other coloration somewhere on the body. This was not always the case; indeed, they used to be common (even though they have no equivalent among the wild cats). However, superstitions linking black cats to witches or simply regarding black cats as evil/unlucky were sufficiently influential that all-black cats were bred virtually out of existence, and often just killed on sight.

The reason a cat can get through such narrow spaces – so long as the cat can get her/his head through, the rest of the body should fit – is that, unlike us, the cat lacks a true collar bone. S/he can thus manipulate the shoulders in ways that we can only dream of!

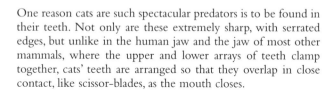

One reason cats are such spectacular predators is to be found in their teeth. Not only are these extremely sharp, with serrated edges, but unlike in the human jaw and the jaw of most other mammals, where the upper and lower arrays of teeth clamp together, cats' teeth are arranged so that they overlap in close contact, like scissor-blades, as the mouth closes.

An adult cat can jump upwards to a height seven times her/his own height.

The life expectancy of a mongrel cat is on average longer than that of a purebred one – yet one more reason why you should get new cats from your local animal shelter! However, the average life expectancy of a cat living in the wild is dramatically shorter than the equivalent cat who has a home: about three years.

The adult human skeleton has 206 bones (not counting the clusters of minute sesamoid bones in the tendons of the thumb, etc.), with children having rather more: babies are born with about 300 bones, but many fuse during the infant's growth. The adult cat, even though far smaller than a human, is bonier: s/he has about 290 bones – and 517 separate muscles to go with them.

A cat's normal body temperature is 38.6°C (101.5°F). By comparison, that of a human is 36.9°C (98.4°F). At rest, a cat's heart beats about 110–140 times per minute, or roughly twice as fast as a human's.